Tales of Languedoc

Tales of Languedoc

from the South of France

Samuel Jacques Brun

With an Introduction by
Harriet W. Preston

Illustrations by
Ernest C. Peixotto

Hippocrene Books, Inc.
New York

Hippocrene Books, Inc. edition, 1999.

Originally published in 1899 by The Macmillan Company.

For information, address:
HIPPOCRENE BOOKS, INC.
171 Madison Avenue
New York, NY 10016

Library of Congress Cataloging-in-Publication Data:
Brun, Samuel Jacques.
  [Tales of Languedoc]
  Tales of Languedoc from the South of France / Samuel Jacques Brun ;
with an introduction by Harriet W. Preston ; illustrations by Ernest
C.   Peixotto.
        p.   cm.
  Summary: A collection of folktales from the South of France,
presented as if being narrated by different storytellers, including
"The Story of the Three Strong Men," " A Blind Man's Story," and "The
Marriage of Monsieur Arcanvel."
    ISBN 0-7818-0715-8
      1.   Tales—France. [1. Folklore—France.]   I. Peixotto, Ernest
C.   , 1869-1940, ill. II. Title.
  PZ8. 1 .B833Tal   1998
  398. 2' 0944'8—dc21   98-27817
                                                     CIP
                                                     AC

Printed in the United States of America

To the Memory of

THE STORY TELLERS

Preface

THE "TALES OF LANGUEDOC" are drawn from a fund of stories, sayings, and traditions, which came to me by birthright, along with the ancient Bible, the tall clock, and other heirlooms, carrying with them about the same sense of exclusive ownership. Whatever may have been their origin in common folk-lore, they formed an important part of the conviviality of the ancestral hearth from an early date, and for several generations have taken on the personality of the different narrators; so that, in their present form, I have come to regard them as my heritage of the unwritten literature of my native land — a heritage that has brought with it a responsibility in view of succession; for, to survive in a new world and with a new generation, oral traditions must take on a permanent form, verbal narration must be written, and the vernacular find an equivalent in the colloquial expressions of another language. To attempt so difficult a thing with only my own resources would be presumptuous. Besides the indelible impressions of a youth passed with a race of story-tellers, I have fortunately been able to command help of a more tangible nature, without which the collection would not be complete.

The sole survivor of the story-tellers has, with much labor, furnished me with his own manuscripts, delineating the tales in the vernacular, and supplying the connecting links.

With this material I have worked to combine and embody, as in a composite picture, the caste and coloring given by the different narrators, calling to aid an able artist, Mr. Ernest Peixotto, to supply in a measure the loss of scenery and associations, and the acting that went so far to supplement the original version.

The difficulty of rendering the coarse picturesqueness of a language so rich in metaphor and so free in its range of figurative expressions could only be partially met by the use of slang and vulgarisms, which it is hoped will be considered pardonable. The rhymes and quatrains, with the sonorous ring of the vernacular, which sets itself to meter so easily, can have no equivalent in English.

My aim in working out this English version has been to give the spirit of the Languedoc, and to do justice to the original, rather than to reach any standard of scientific or literary value.

Soulless as the tales must seem to those initiated in the magic of story-telling, yet practice proves them capable of exerting a spell over the children and having some interest for lovers of folk-lore — so much so, that the author is encouraged to invite to the hearth a wider circle.

To the critic the collection will appear full of anachronisms and inconsistencies. Legend and romance are unduly seasoned with the moral and didactic to the taste of a sterner sect of Huguenots; the medieval and modern are brought face to face; and fact and fable join hands, regardless of rhyme or reason. Yet all this only rendered them real to those of the ancestral hearth, who knew no sharp lines between the past and present, and who lived on the borderland of the fabulous.

To my own fireside I owe, in some measure, the inspiration which may be found in these tales; and to my wife, with whom I discussed the idioms of the *langue d'oc*, the apt rendering of the vernacular.

With gratefulness I acknowledge the deep obligation I owe to my uncle, M. Clément Brun, of Fontanès, France, for furnishing me with his written version of most of these tales, as he had them from the lips of my great-grandfather at the beginning of the second quarter of this century, and for the suggestion to make of the stories a connected whole.

My acknowledgments are also due to Dr. Ewald Flügel, Professors Melville Best Anderson, and Henry Burrowes Lathrop, of Stanford University, for the great interest they have taken in these tales, and the encouragement given to this undertaking.

SAMUEL JACQUES BRUN.

Leland Stanford Jr. University, September 1st, 1896.

Contents

LIST OF DRAWINGS

List of Drawings

Introduction

IT is very nearly forty years since the first publication, at Avignon, of Frederick Mistral's " Mireio " marked the brilliant opening of one of the most noteworthy literary movements of this century. A new poet of unmistakable genius, producing at the first bound a work of epic proportions, with a theme of singular freshness, and in a hitherto neglected Latin dialect,—it will be long before the reading world receives another such sensation! And the wonder grew, as it became apparent that the new singer was only one, although the leader, of a tuneful choir, with a common inspiration, a close organization, and a distinct and serious literary purpose. If that purpose has been but imperfectly fulfilled, in so far as it regarded the claim of the rustic modern Provençal to rank as a separate and long-descended language, in other respects the daring promise of the first "felibre" has been richly kept. They had actually struck a vein hitherto unworked in letters, and the mine of poetic and picturesque material to which it led, has been yielding steadily for a generation, and shows no signs as yet of failure. The men of the early school, many of whom have already passed away, were born and bred in the romantic period, and idealized upon principle their pictures of Provençal life and scenery.

Then came Alphonse Daudet, the most sane and sympathetic of realists, no less a patriot in the best sense of the term, because he was also a citizen of the world, who dared, in "Les Lettres de Mon Moulin," and the immortal "Numa Roumestan," to depict the humor and confess the limitations, as well as chant the glories, of the South of France.

Between them, they have succeeded in making their fascinating country a familiar haunt of the fancy, even to those who have never seen it; and we know the men and women of Gard and Var, Vaucluse and the Bouches du Rhône as we know our next of kin. We have roamed their fields and gathered their fruit, eaten at their tables, knelt in their churches, and shouted at their banquets. We have a lively interest in all their concerns, from the gravest to the most trivial, and have come long since to care less for the manner of their native speech than for the substance of the news which they have to give us of themselves. We are only too glad, therefore, to have the part played by the humble kindred of Mirabeau in the great Revolution, illustrated by Madame Janvier's graceful translation of Felix Gras's "Reds of the Midi," and to make acquaintance with the fireside tales and local traditions on which the children of Gard are brought up, in the singularly clear, animated, and idiomatic English of M. Samuel Jacques Brun.

It was a happy thought of Mr. Brun's to give a permanent form to the half-dozen extravagant but highly entertaining *viva voce* naratives which had constituted for generations a sort of heirloom in his own family; and their publication seems peculiarly opportune just now, when the taste for story-telling pure and simple, without any oblique purpose or appended moral, has so remarkably revived. No such feast for the juvenile imagination has been provided since the Brothers Grimm collected the " Märchen " of Germany; and the scientific student of folk-lore may welcome the opportunity now offered him of comparing the nursery legends of Northern and Southern Europe from his own serious point of view. But the great merit and charm for the general reader, in these ingenuous " Contes Bleus " of Languedoc will be found in their broad and beaming humor and their intensely dramatic quality. Even the tales of Hans Christian Andersen, and the marvelous " Jungle Book " appear slow, subtle, and tortuous beside the breathless movement and almost brutal directness of these. Character, as in the delightful fable of the " Three Strong Men," is drawn in true child-fashion, with the fewest and blackest lines; but the effect is immense. There is an endless succession of thrilling incidents and adventures, preposterous in themselves, it may be, but related with the most imposing conviction, and rendered quite credible for the moment by the ease of their sequence, and the rapidity with which they pass. Inconsistencies are reconciled and anachronisms overborne by the strong vitality of the perennial story, which, as it is handed down from father to son, adopts and retains something from each period without losing its identity, and often reflects, in quaint association with the most modern views and impressions, the ruling passion of a long-past time—the Huguenot's hatred and distrust of the priest; the exulting contempt of the first republican era for courtiers and kings. Now and then, perhaps, the sentiment is less antiquated than it appears, and points to some unchangeable idiosyncrasy of race. The exceedingly rude treatment accorded to the gentle bride in the story of "Monsieur Arcanvel" might seem like a survival from the dark ages, but for our recollection of the complacency with which good Tante Portal in "Numa Roumestan" is made to quote the current Provençal proverb: "*Les femmes ne sont pas des genss.*"

Very rarely, as in the droll story of "How Anglas Became a Marquis, or the Ants, the Ducks, and Flies," a certain flourish is made at the outset of a precept to be inculcated—in this case the duty of kindness and consideration to the humblest of God's creatures. But here, as always, the story is so much better even than the moral, that the latter falls rather into abeyance.

The main lessons conveyed by the fireside tales of Languedoc are those benignant and encouraging, if elementary ones—those which appeal so forcibly to a child's sense of justice, and are none the less grateful to the reader of experience because they show a refreshing disparity with the average results of life — that the bravest youth will win the best and fairest bride, without reference to original differences of condition; that the virtuous poor man will inherit and enjoy the estates of the malign millionaire; and the bold, bad boy who has maltreated his brother will be humbled in due course of time and handed over to the relentless magnanimity of his junior; in short, that every good deed is bound to receive a tangible reward, even in this present evil world, and every wrong a triumphant righting.

The time-worn elder may shake his head officially over such flattering promises, but his juvenile auditory will be clamoring loudly meanwhile to hear the story read again; and that, after all, is the true test of excellence in such matters.

HARRIET WATERS PRESTON.

October 1st, 1896.

✠ ✠

My Grandfather's
Tour of France.

✠ ✠

My Grandfather's Tour of France

DURING the long winter evenings of my youth, my grandfather used to amuse us and keep us awake by telling stories of all sorts, but the one which we liked best was the account of a journey that he had taken when a young man before his marriage.

Travelling in those days was very different from what it is now. The middle class had no private carriages; the lords, and high dignitaries of the church, travelled in lumbering vehicles of their own over abominable roads; the industrial, the bourgeois, travelled on horseback, and the rest on foot. To be sure the mail coach carried three or four passengers, but that was too expensive for any but the nobles, the clergy, and the government officials. The pedestrians, and they were few, indeed, for most people staid at home, were *"compagnons"* or journeymen-joiners, saddlers, masons, carpenters, blacksmiths, and others, who tramped about to see the country and returned home with the prestige of a traveller. *"Faire son tour de France"* it was called.

However skillful a craftsman the "*compagnon*" might be, he was not considered up in his trade unless he had made his "*tour de France,*" and though he had travelled ever so little the most stupid fellow in the universe was all right if he had gone a few miles away from home. Some went to Galician, others to Uzès, a few went to Lyons, and when one, perchance, went to Paris, then you should have seen how proud he was, and heard the lies he told. Ah, that one knew it all!

Almost all left home well dressed, with sack well-filled and some money in pocket; they returned lean and empty, in tattered summer clothes in the middle of winter, a few rags tied in a handkerchief, shoes out at the sole, a shock of unkempt hair, and as much money as there is in my eye. But, in spite of all this, look out! they had been to Lyons! Well, the customs of the times were such!

Those, who like my grandfather had been to distant countries for their education, were very rare, and often they had for travelling companions the tradesmen above mentioned or some soldiers returning home from their discharge.

You must understand that such a journey lasted many months and that, from time to time, the traveller had to rest. My grandfather improved those days in visiting places of interest in the towns where he tarried as he passed through. Thus he saw many sights, had many adventures, heard many tales, and it was all this

that he used to relate to us winter evenings by the large
fire-place of the ancestral dwelling.

My brother and I sat on each side of the hearth under
the mantel of the great kitchen chimney, watching the
slow burning log, hearing the sizz of the pot hung on
the crane, and listening for hours to the stories of my
white-haired grandfather.

I shall let my grandfather speak and be only the
scribe taking down the story as faithfully as my memory
will allow.

"When I was young I had a great leaning toward
an education. I remember going to school and taking
great delight in reading the two or three books which
were all the teacher had, and in the lessons in geography of France, on the customs of the people, and a
good deal about distant countries. These things interested me so much, that the desire to see for myself the
things he told us about increased as I grew older, and
when out of my teens, I ventured to speak to my father
of my great desire to travel. My father was much
surprised at first and a little annoyed; but, as he was
exceedingly intelligent, he soon realized that a trip to
distant provinces might be a great benefit to me through
life—a serious journey, of course, not a frivolous trip,—
so he took me to his room, and very impressively gave
me all the injunctions which his parental duty required.

"He told me what my conduct should be towards my

fellowmen, especially my fellow travellers—he cautioned me against being out late, and warned me of wicked companions and highwaymen—he gave me much other counsel to which I gave little heed at the time,—like any other youngster, but which, I confess, was to me of great value during my journey, as well as in after life.

"'To encourage you in well-doing,' added my father, 'I will tell you what happened to a young man of the Camargue—you will see that good conduct and kindness often receive their reward on this earth.'"

✤　✤

How Young Anglas Became a Marquis, or the Story of the Ducks, the Ants, and the Flies.

✤　✤

How Young Anglas Became a Marquis

NOT far from Aiguemorte, on the Mediterranean sea, lived a rich peasant named Anglas. His farm was one of the finest in the fertile region of the Lower Rhone, and was known far and wide as, 'The Tour of Anglas.'

On this domain he lived with his son, a promising young man, upon whom he had bestowed great care.

Young Anglas had finished school, and was eager to take a trip to Paris. Ambitious as such an undertaking was for his country-folk, the father had granted the young man's desire, and furnished a handsome outfit for the journey. A fine young horse from the Camargue, snow white, with head alert, tail sweeping the ground, nimble as a lean cat! He could leap a twelve-foot ditch at a bound, and the rider was fearless as the steed was swift.

A fine appearance they made on the morn of the departure, the shining white palfrey and handsome young rider. The father could not help exclaiming, as he viewed the youth from top to toe, admiring his black hair, hazel eyes, pearly teeth, and self-reliant manner: "What a fine fellow; not many can equal him!" Then he added, with a shade of sadness: "May God bless him on his journey, and may he return to me a man of experience, yet as pure and good as he is now."

When the horse and rider were lost to sight, the old man fell a prey to sad reflections; a tear moistened his eye, and as he entered his house he said: "Alas, what awaits him in his travels? Were I with him I might direct and protect him; but ignorant as he is of the hardships of travel, the temptations of the world and of evil companions, abandoned to himself, what will become of him?" And day by day, as he followed his son in his wanderings northward, he thought only of the perils he might encounter, and his heart remained a prey to the griefs of separation.

From the young man's point of view all appeared very different. He had heard so much about it from his friends who had taken the trip that he was burning with desire to see and learn; so it was not with reluctance that he quitted the farm, on that eventful morning, mounted his pawing steed, gay as a goldfinch, and dashed out into the world, scarcely looking back to see his father, who stood waving adieus until he was out of sight.

In holiday mood, the young man went on his way. The sights he saw and the adventures he met with will make a wonderful story, so let us follow him.

His way at first led along dikes and ditches, through marshes and among many ponds and lakes. He passed over bridges, across islets, and forded the shallow waters

as he pursued his course.   Little villages sprang up as
waymarks.   He had passed several before the close of the
first day,—Bramasec, Canaveira, Servilla, and was nearing La Fossa, when something happened.   The white
dust in the middle of the road suddenly became alive, a
black moving mass confronted him.   He stopped short,
very much frightened, and found to his great surprise
that the road was covered, as far as he could see, with
ducks.   Ducks are plenty in that region, and they often
migrate from one lake to another, either swimming or
flying; but these were ducklings, in pin-feathers, and
could not fly at all, so the traveller was brought to a
standstill before this army of slow waddlers.   "He walks
like a duck," is often said of a clumsy walker; and, with
the way blocked by these slow, awkward creatures, what
to do was the question.

While Anglas was debating, up came a mother of the
flock, and said to him, in her *patois*, "Gentle knight, do
no harm either to me or my flock, and I may some day
do you a service."

"My father," said Anglas, "has too often taught me
to harm no one for me not to heed his advice; I will
do you no harm;" so saying, he spurred his horse, which,
quick as a deer, leaped the ditch to the right, and followed the dike.   From this vantage ground he looked
back on the ducks.   The road was full of them; as far
as the eye could reach there was nothing but ducks.
Reaching the end of the dike of the ditch, he rode on

the high dikes of the Rhone, and the road was yet full
of them. At last, about sundown, he passed the last
ones, and, as he wished to spend the night at Galician,
at the house of a friend, he decided to ford the lake.

The horse and rider, gliding over the waters of the
lake, was a scene for a painter. The superb animal held
his head proudly high, while his long, flowing mane
trailed the water, and his waving tail floated out behind.
He seemed to scarcely sink in the water for fear of drench-
ing his rider. Thus they safely crossed the lake, and
reached, by nightfall, the house of his friend.

Here Anglas met with a hearty welcome. His friend
did not expect him, but was greatly pleased to see him.

After the usual greetings, a good supper and a night's
rest, he set out next day as cheerily as on the first of his
journey.

He did not mention to his friend his meeting with the
ducks nor his conversation with the mother duck. It
was too natural in those regions to meet ducks, and as to
his conversation with the leader of the flock, he attached
to it too little importance.

Thanking his friend warmly, he set out for Garon,
thence toward Jonquières, crossed the Rhone on the sus-
pension-bridge at Beaucaire, visiting Tarascon and her
Tarasque, which is neither man nor beast, but a creature
of whose historic fame you may sometimes learn. From
Tarascon he went to Avignon, and saw the castles of the
Popes.

A month later, we find him in the vicinity of Vienne, in Dauphiny, at the foot of a steep grade known as the Grade of Tarare. The sun hardly pierces the clouds, his horse, which has been trotting since leaving the inn, is set to a walk. He is cheerful, happy, and, so far, satisfied with his journey.

The road makes a sharp bend a little higher up. When he reaches this bend, he stops short, and, this time, very much frightened.

His horse sprang to one side, and, had he not been a good horseman, he would have been thrown off. But he is not a man, after all, to lose his wits; he pats the horse's neck, speaks reassuringly to him, and faces the seeming danger.

The road appeared to be flowing with blood, as if poured out from the hill-top. "Good gracious!" he exclaimed, "a whole army must have been massacred on yonder hill! What does all this mean?"

While thus guessing, the blood reached his horse's feet and he saw that it was only a colony of red ants pouring down the road, like an avalanche. No doubt, they were on their way to a change of climate, and fast they went, too, unlike the flock of ducks previously met.

One of the mother ants left the ranks, and came towards him, and said, in her language, "Horseman, gentle horseman, do no harm either to me or my little ones, and we may some day render you a service."

Young Anglas, faithful to his father's admonitions,

granted her request, and, as in the case of the ducks, left the highway, went down precipices, climbed steep hills, crossed woods and ravines, at the risk of his life. Two or three times he came near the road to follow it again, but found it full of ants, and was obliged to turn away. At last, about sunset, he was able to take the road, and reached, by nightfall, a town.

The next day, and the day following, he pursued his way. observing, and taking notes of the points of interest. Two weeks after his encounter with the ants we find him on the banks of the Seine, in the vicinity of Melum.

On that day the sky was overcast, it had rained during the night, the atmosphere was thick and muggy, not a breath of air was stirring. Toward ten o'clock, the sun pierced the clouds, and the heat was depressing.

He was walking his horse, whose white coat was covered with foam. Young Anglas was mopping his brow, and exclaiming, "Whew, what a hot day!" when the sun hid again behind a cloud. The cloud proved to be a swarm of flies, and they soon surrounded him. They were everywhere,—overhead, at his horse's feet, in the road, on the trees. Although in the swamps of the Camargue, near his home, flies are unusually thick, never had he seen so many of them.

He had stopped his horse, and was thinking what to do, when a mother fly came out of the swarm, and said to him, this time in pretty good French, "Horseman, gentle horseman, do no harm to me or my little ones,

and I may some day render you a service." As this was
the third time the request had been made, he was somewhat surprised; but, still remembering his father's injunctions, he left the main road, went across meadows
and plowed land, up and down many hills, to avoid
hurting any of them.

When he took the road again, all the flies had passed,
and not one of them had been killed by accident or other-
wise by his horse or himself.

At last, at the end of a certain time, he arrived in
Paris, in good health, high spirits, and promising himself
the pleasure of visiting every nook and corner of the great
capital of France.

Far was he from foreseeing what awaited him. Hardly
had he alighted from his horse at the inn where he had
decided to stay, when the innkeeper said to him, "No
doubt, you have come to compete like all the other
youths,—the more, the merrier!—and why not? At
your time of life you must do like the rest."

Surprised to be thus addressed, he replied, "I do not
know what you mean. Is there a race, a contest, a competition of some sort? I know nothing at all about it."

"Yes, yes," said the innkeeper, "I will tell you all
about it; let us have our dinner."

At table he found a great many youths, come from all
parts of France. Each one related what he had done, as
well as some things he had not done. Many a lie was
told and much boasting indulged in. Young Anglas,

from the corner of the table, was all ears to listen, and, finally, learned what the innkeeper meant by a competition. It would take too long to tell all that was said, but, in short, it was this:

The king, while boating on the Seine, had used his pocket-handkerchief (kings are human, like other people); drawing it from his pocket, the keys of the royal coffers had fallen into the water.

At once everybody was set in motion to find them; the boatmen of the Seine, the sailors of the ocean, the fishermen of the country.

For over a month they had dived, fished, and dredged daily, but in vain. The keys could not be found. The king was in despair. He needed money—kings always need money—and, without his keys, the royal treasury could not be opened.

Then, in a moment of great impatience, the king caused to be announced that he would give his daughter in marriage to any one who should bring him the keys within twenty-four hours. The twenty-four hours was to begin the day after young Anglas arrived,—at ten o'clock in the morning.

You may imagine what a hurly-burly Paris was in! On what a scale preparations were made! All the boats were let for their weight in gold. All the fishermen from all the ports of France had come. Every man who owned a boat on the French rivers was on the spot; so the commotion and noise was beyond description.

At the appointed time, all Paris and a great part of the surrounding populace were on the banks of the Seine. The innkeeper and young Anglas were in the crowd, but only as spectators. All were eager to know who the happy mortal would be whom chance would favor as finder of the keys. The king himself and his whole court had come to join the throng.

All day long they fished, they dredged, they jostled one another, but without results. At nightfall the crowd dispersed, the king and his court returned to the palace; but all were bent on returning next day to try again their luck.

In the evening at the table each one related his exploits. One had felt something under his harpoon and thought he had them, another had seen a shining thing in his net and had his hopes raised, but it proved to be only a piece of glass, again another told of great things he had seen and done; when a youth from the middle of the table addressed young Anglas, saying: " You have not tried; do you believe the keys will come in your pocket by magic? If you don't search you can't have them; ' all the craft is in the catching.'"

He replied: " I did not come to Paris for this purpose, I knew nothing about the lost keys, it is the innkeeper who told me of it first, and he also accompanied me to the Seine as a mere spectator; and when I saw that jostling, quarrelling crowd, and heard the uproar, I remarked to myself that no one could fish out those keys;

so you will not have a competitor in me.   To-morrow I
will do as I did to-day, I will watch you."

From the middle of the table a tall stout lad spoke up
loud enough to be heard all over the room: "Fellows, I
distrust those who are so discreet and say little!   Often
they work underhand and all their modesty is just put
on to mask their plans,"—then suddenly rising before

them all—"I prefer men who say frankly what they
think; so to the boldest the king's daughter!"

All eyes were turned toward young Anglas, even a
few spoke roughly of him, and had not the innkeeper
interfered by announcing that it was bedtime they would
have insulted him.

Poor Anglas retired to his room much grieved at what had been said about him. He was pacing the floor in a gloomy mood when he heard three taps on his window pane. He stopped short, said to himself: "What does this mean, is the room haunted? Ghosts would not surely come to the third story," and he resumed his walk.

Tap, tap, tap, was again heard at the window pane. He approached, opened it and what was his surprise to find a large duck who said to him: "Knight, gentle knight, you hurt neither me nor my little ones, I have come to render you a service in return."

"Why, I do not need anything," said Anglas, "thank you just the same."

"Well," replied the duck, "I heard that the king lost his keys and I wish to dive and get them for you. Everybody is in bed, all is quiet, the moon shines bright, come to the banks of the Seine and within an hour I will give you the lost keys."

A ray of hope crossed his mind, he took his hat, went noiselessly out of the house and betook himself to the Seine.

What he saw was well worth a painter's brush; the pale rays of the moon lighting the Seine, the trees casting here and there soft shadows, and on the waters of the swift stream, arranged in battalions, thousands of ducks only waiting the mother's signal to dive for the keys.

When Anglas appeared the mother said:

"Children, carefully examine the mud.   Ready?
Dive!"

Heads down, tails up!   Down they all went at once
and staid so long that Anglas thought them drowned.
At last they all came up together.

"Have you found anything?" said the mother.

"Nothing! nothing!" shouted they in concert.

"Be not discouraged," said the mother; "the current
is here very strong and the keys may have been carried
to yonder bend."

She rested her ducklings a while and then gave the
signal for a new plunge.   Heads down, tails up!—and
the water closed in wavelets over the flock.   Ten thousand bills sifted the fine mud of the river-bend.   They
remained longer than the first time.

Then—Whizz!   The fleet emerged and with a toss of
the head each duck flung the water from his feathers
and from every throat rose the exultant cry:

"We have them! we have them!"

The mother duck took the keys from the one that
found them, placed them in Anglas's hand, and before
he had time to thank her they were gone.

Left alone with the precious keys in his hand, the
young man was filled with joy.   He returned to his hotel,
shut himself in his room and tried to sleep, but in vain.

Morning came; he hastened to see the innkeeper and
inform him of his find.   The good man exclaimed, in
astonishment:

"You have found the keys! you are the luckiest youth in the world! To-morrow you will be the king's son-in-law! Come quickly with me." And both went to hail the king, who was getting ready to go to the Seine.

"My king," said the innkeeper, "this youth has found these keys,—see whether they are yours."

The king took the keys, examined them carefully, and said:

"They are mine."

He inserted them in the lock and opened the royal treasury. Then, turning toward Anglas: "You shall wed my daughter."

In one hour all Paris knew that the keys had been found, and who the finder was. The tall lad who had hinted that Anglas was mum, said to his friends:

"I told you so! Look out for those uncommunicative fellows! Perhaps at the very moment I was talking to you he had the keys in his pocket."

Another said: "He was not seen in any boat; he watched us the whole day. I don't understand it."

A third added "No one knows where he hails from,—his mother may be a witch. Did you not see how queer he acted as he sat at the end of the table and listened all agape to everything that was said, hardly answering a question, so shy and innocent? Oh, he had not come to compete! Then, whack! we are left,—that's always the way,—'The fool will not be foiled.' Well, 'There's no use crying over spilled milk.'"

The Parisians thronged the streets to see the lucky fellow who had found the keys—all Paris was in a turmoil. Meanwhile very grave matters occupied the king and his court.

Most likely, if Anglas had fished out the keys under the king's very nose, he would not have gone back on his word; but the courtiers suspected magic. The keys had not been found at evening, and in the morning this young man brought them to the king; so they must have been found in the night. The king and his courtiers would like to know all about it, but Anglas held to the king's decree, which merely said whosoever should find the keys within twenty-four hours should marry his daughter,—and he kept his own counsel.

Courtiers are often envious; besides, most of them had sons whom they would have most willingly married to the king's daughter. They took counsel, and said to the king:

"Sire, your decree was given out in a moment of impatience; so, in your wisdom, you may annul it for the honor of your crown and the happiness of your daughter. This young man is entirely unknown to any of us; we know not from whence he comes; a mystery surrounds the finding of the keys, and rumor has it that a fairy gave them to him. We are all of the opinion that he should be put to another trial, to find out whether he is a magician."

The king allowed himself to be persuaded, and asked how they proposed to try him.

A courtier with a long white beard, sunken eyes and hooked nose, said:

"If the king will believe me, he will have mixed a large heap of wheat, with equal parts of sand, and will give the young man three days to separate the wheat from the sand."

All the courtiers exclaimed: "Good! Capital!" and the king agreed to it.

"In this there can be no magic," said the old man. "He shall be left with the task in a room by himself, and not by night, either."

So said, so done. The whole day wheat and sand were carted to one of the upper rooms of the Bastille, and they informed Anglas that if, in three days, he had separated the wheat from the sand, the king's daughter should be his wife.

Poor fellow; on hearing this his spirits fell; he sank upon a bench, quite faint. He thought a great while, with his head upon his hands, while saying to himself:

"All hope is lost; I shall have to return as I came. That, however, would not pain me so much, for I had not expected such a marriage; but on my father's account I am more sorry. Poor father, how little you know the trials of your son!"

As he was saying this, he felt something biting his

leg. He turned up his trousers and saw a large ant, which said to him:

"Horseman, gentle horseman, you did no harm to me or my little ones, I have come to render you a service. I heard that the king's courtiers had spoiled your chance of getting the king's daughter, by imposing on you a task that fifty men could not do in a month. I will do the work for you. To-night my little ones and I will come on the roof of the Bastille. As soon as you are alone, open the window for us, and you shall see how quickly the work will be done. Farewell until to-morrow."

The king, by his chamberlain, informed Anglas that they would send for him at eight o'clock in the morning; that at noon they would fetch him out for dinner, and return him to his work at two o'clock; at six they would fetch him again, but that no one was to enter his room and disturb him in his work.

The following day at the appointed time, he was taken to the Bastille. They made him wind through corridors, ascend stair-cases, cross rooms, which the door-keepers opened and closed with enormous keys, and, finally, after many turns, he was ushered into the room which contained the heap of sand and wheat. "There is your task," said the guide. The door was closed, the lock grated, and Anglas was left alone.

The mother ant, on leaving Anglas, went quickly to gather her little ones. They crossed Paris under cover

of the night, reached the Bastille, and climbed to the roof unseen by any one. To be sure, some Parisians had noticed the roof all red, but took it for the reflection of the sunrise.

When Anglas was left alone, he hastened to open the window. The ants poured in silently and noiselessly. The mother ant formed them in rows, so that they could work without interfering with each other, and gave the word of command.

The young ants set to work with an alacrity seldom seen, even in ants.

By noon they had the work half done; they rested just long enough to eat, and went on with their work. Long before six o'clock they were through. Quickly and silently they left the room, climbed over the roof, lodged in between the tiles, awaiting the dead of night to cross Paris.

When the chamberlain came towards six o'clock to fetch Anglas, he inquired of the young man how he was getting along, adding: "I hope you are not discouraged."

"Not at all," replied the youth, "little cause for it, since I am through."

"Through!" exclaimed the officer," through? No, that can't be. Let me see."

They went in. The chamberlain was dumbfounded. On one side was the heap of wheat, yellow and clean, as if just from a pigeon's crop, and on the other side was the sand.

He hastened to inform the king and courtiers, who, with faces as long as their sleeves, eyed one another aghast. With crest-fallen mien, they muttered between their teeth: "How has he done this feat! Fifty men could not have done it in a month, and this fellow has done it in a day!" The mystery was greater than before.

Said the one who had devised the test: "It is noised that this fellow is a wizard, and were I the king, I would certainly not give him my daughter before knowing more about him. All the courtiers said that the gentleman was right, and had they a daughter, they would hesitate to give her to him.

Anglas had meanwhile gone to his hotel to await the king's decision. Racked by many conflicting emotions, he scarcely slept that night.

Early in the morning, he came down stairs and met the innkeeper, who said to him: "Young man, I see you are very unhappy; it is unfortunate for you that you have no friends at court. After what you have done, the king's daughter should be yours. Had you been one of the courtier's sons, she would now be your wife. I shall be much surprised if they do not invent some pretext to cheat you out of your right yet. Jealousy is cruel, and stoops to anything. Note what I say, young man."

Anglas calmly, but manfully, replied: "I am here to see it through,"

At ten o'clock the court met to deliberate and see what should be done. Each courtier did his best to calumniate the youth and to flatter the king; but his majesty cut their speeches short by saying:

"Gentlemen, so far I have followed your advice, now hear what I have decided of my own account.

"I will choose twelve girls of the same size, same age, and in looks as nearly like my daughter as possible. They shall be dressed in white, and shall stand together in my presence, yours, and the young man's. If he guesses which one is my daughter, he shall have her for his wife. Such is my good pleasure."

All the courtiers found the scheme excellent. They perhaps did not think so, but, as servile flatterers, they highly approved of it; hoping secretly that they might disconcert him by their presence, so that he would not guess right.

The test was to take place on the next day at ten o'clock, and rendezvous was given Anglas at the palace of the king.

Our youth felt very uneasy on hearing this. Country bred, as he was, the idea of court manners and court society seemed very formidable. To stand in the presence of the king, and handsome lords and ladies in full dress, and to face the twelve young damsels, who would, no doubt, think him very awkward, was no small ordeal. So his heart was beating to breaking when he came into the presence of the brilliant company.

His embarrassment was somewhat relieved by the king, who said: "My young friend, come near me, and if within an hour you point out to me and my court the one of the twelve young ladies who is my daughter, she shall be your wife; I pledge you my kingly word."

Young Anglas made no reply, but was thinking that his chances of guessing right were small, having never seen the young princess before, when something tickled his ear and a small voice whispered:

"Horseman, gentle horseman, you hurt neither me nor my little flies; now I have come to render you a service. Watch me carefully. I will alight on the nose of the king's daughter. She will brush me off with her fan. Pay close attention."

With a flight she is on the nose of the princess. With her fan the damsel brushes her off. She goes out by the key-hole to get a breath of air, then flies to Anglas's ear.

"Did you notice her?" said she; "well, watch again."

Once more she is on the nose of her highness, once more she is brushed off. She flies out of the room for a while, and finally alights on the window-sill, passes her fore feet over her head, and, with her hind feet, smooths her wings, apparently joyous to be of use to the kind young man. Then, for the third time, she tickles the royal nose, and, for the third time, she is brushed off with the fan.

Returning to Anglas, she inquired if he was sure of

picking out the princess. "Yes, yes; many thanks," said Anglas.

"Well," said the king, "which do you say is my daughter? The happiness of your life is in this choice."

"If I choose aright may I kiss her hand?"

"Certainly, my boy," replied the king.

Anglas bowed, went straight to the king's daughter, knelt before her, and printed a kiss upon her fingers.

Greatly surprised, the king exclaimed in a firm voice, "Kiss her on both cheeks, she is your bride."

The young man accepted the privilege with perfect composure. The princess, blushing, gave one of her sweetest smiles, and the courtiers offered their warmest congratulations.

The king bowed himself away, entered his private apartment, and summoned Anglas before him.

"Tell me," said the king, "who are you, and rom whence you come?"

Anglas, with a candor and frankness that pleased the king, told his whole story. His majesty, glad to have found such a wise and good man, gave orders to receive Anglas at the palace at once, and for his father to be summoned to Paris.

Proud and happy, the father came, rejoicing that his advice had borne such fruit.

The king conferred the title of Marquis on Anglas the day of the wedding, and gave him large estates, fine castles, horses, and equipages in plenty.   And this is how Young Anglas became Marquis.

The cock crew, the story ended, and my father remarked:

> " Caoù ten lou dré camin, caðu és bon, juste, aïmablé,
> Caoù faï pa tor a rés, qués umen, charitablé,
> Sé sus terra das omès és pa récoumpensa,
> Lou boun Dïou lou survéïa é l'abandouna pa." *

* Whosoever keeps the narrow path, is kind, just, and true ; wrongs no one, is humane, charitable, if on this Earth he receives no reward, God who watches over him will not forsake him.

WHEN bedtime came we retired,—my father, sad and thoughtful, I full of plans for the future, and jubilant over the prospect of setting out next morning. We were all up by daylight. My mother had prepared all that I needed for my journey,—linen, hat, shoes, haversack, iron-shod stick, and sundry other useful articles,—while my father had provided me liberally with money. I kissed them good-bye, and off I went.

This was on Monday morning; the weather was unpropitious, a thick mist enveloped the house and trees, but, withal, my heart was light, and I felt supremely happy.

When I reached the two hills known as Lous Dous Pio, I was met by two men of a neighboring village. They addressed me very pleasantly, and with them I had some instructive conversation. I learned for the first time that off one's own line of thought one can learn a great deal from even the humblest of men. These two were charcoal-burners, on their way to Quian, to see some standing wood for sale.

In the course of my talk with them I learned that to prevent the denuding of forests, and to maintain the rainfall about constant, the law prevents the cutting of more than a twentieth of the woodland each year; so that the second growth on the first cutting shall be nineteen years old when the last twentieth is being removed.

The China-Vender of Quissac

ABOUT three o'clock in the afternoon, we reached the little town of Quissac, and found to our surprise, a great crowd gathered on the public square. There seemed to be some unusual excitement; for as we approached, we saw a woman jumping about like a lunatic, and complaining loudly to the authorities of some men who stood there laughing at her, and seeming to enjoy the situation.

Once a week, in the little villages, there is a market day. Merchants of all kinds go and spread out their wares in the streets, and the peasants come to buy their weekly provision.

It was market-day, and a china-vender had brought a donkey-load of her wares, and spread them out on the ground. She had a very good assortment. The women gathered around her, and she was driving a brisk trade. The donkey, tired from carrying the load, was eating hay a few feet away. A group of good-for-nothing idlers stood looking on,— one finds them in a crowd the world over,— the loafers with more money than brains, and the wag in their midst. These were smoking short-stemmed pipes, and swapping jokes, when the wag said to the others:

"Would you like to have a laugh?"

"Of course," replied they, "and what are you up to?"

"You will see;" and speaking to the crockery woman:

"My good woman, if you will allow me to say two words in your donkey's ear, I will give you twenty-four sous," said he.

"What have you to tell my donkey"? inquired the crockery-vender.

"Oh! not much; but I am sure I will make him happy. It will be no mystery; I shall speak loud enough for all to hear."

"No, no; I won't allow you to do it," replied the vender.

"Why not?" retorted another one; "he is not going to eat your donkey by speaking a few words in his ear, and you will earn twenty-four sous; you had better let him do it."

She very reluctantly gave her consent; and the wag, with his short-stemmed-pipe freshly lighted in his mouth, approached the donkey, inserted the pipe in his ear, and while saying:

"Té, do you know your sister is engaged, and you will soon be at the wedding," he blew his pipe, and the fire fell into the donkey's ear.

The beast jumped, shook its head, flapped its ears, and trampled on the crockery ware. The vender was

wild with rage. She shouted for help; she tore her hair
to see her plates and bowls all broken; she called those
men all sorts of names. They split their sides with
laughter, while the wag coolly said to the good woman:

"Did n't I tell you so? He fairly jumped for joy;
probably he has never been at a wedding before; that is
why it tickled him so."

When the commotion created by the donkey and its
owner had subsided, the crowd slowly dispersed. My
fellow-travelers and I, who had unexpectedly witnessed
the end of this village scene, separated. They looked for
lodgings at the little inn, while I went to the house of an
acquaintance of my father.

Made welcome by the gentleman and his family, I
spent the night at their house.

After supper, a neighbor dropped in for the evening,
or rather dragged himself in; for Master Rinaou was so
old, bowed and paralyzed that he had to lean on two
stout crutches and pull himself along, scraping the stone
floor with his sabots. Thus slowly and painfully he
hitched across the room to the wide arm-chair by the
fireside, threw himself into it all in a heap, hooked his
crutches to one arm, stretched out his lifeless limbs with
his hands and leaned back. Quite unconscious of the
company, he settled himself, sighed and broke out
loudly in self-contempt:

"*Té paouré Mèsté Rinaou, té tombés aqui couma un
paou, ara lèva té, mardienna, coutidienna.*"*

*There, poor Master Rinaou, down you fall like a log; now get up if you can.

The children, however, soon drew him away from himself, by asking for a story.

"Give a story, Mèsté Rinaou; please do, Mèsté Rinaou."

"What can poor Mèsté Rinaou tell you?" said the old man, with a shade of sadness.

"Give Mèsté Règé," said the oldest, a boy of ten.

"Yes, Mèsté Règé, Mèsté Règé," chimed in the other two.

"It is Mèsté Règé you want, Mèsté Règé and Moussu Laouren," said Mèsté Rinaou; "well, listen."

The Adventures of Mèsté Règé

MÈSTÉ Règé lived at Aiguemorte, a small town on the Mediterranean coast, and his friend, Moussu Laouren, lived in the little village of St. Laurent, an hour's walk from Mèsté Règé's house. They used to see each other once a year, when the summer work was over, and, as the hay was in the barn, the grain cut and threshed, the wine-grapes trampled, and the wine in the casks, Mèsté Règé thought of taking some rest and of visiting his friend, Moussu Laouren. Mèsté Règé was in a very happy mood. His crops had been unusually large, especially his wheat-crop. Thirty Camargues horses had trampled for three weeks his threshing-floor. You know how they threshed wheat in the Camargue. The clay floor is covered with upright sheaves closely packed, in the middle stands a strong post firmly anchored to a stone. To this post the half-tamed broncos are tied with long ropes and kept going at a lively pace by a driver with a long lash. As they whirl around the post, they trample over the sheaves, winding up the rope so that the circuits become less and less. When the rope is nearly wound up, the driver turns the post upside down, the rope begins to unwind, the horses go in wider circles until they again reach the edge of the threshing floor. This process is repeated until the straw is evenly trodden and the grain all threshed out.

Well, it was a very prosperous year for Mèsté Règé, and, happy as he was, he did not hesitate long, and his mind was soon made up to go and visit Moussu Laouren. He donned his best suit, exchanged his sabots for a pair of shoes, kissed his wife and children good-bye, took his staff, and set out on his long journey.

By the wayside he knew of an eagle's nest. He had the curiosity to get a peep at it, which is a most danger- ous thing to do, especially when the eaglets are yet in the nest. He hesitated somewhat before going, but decided to satisfy his curiosity and perhaps get a young eaglet to present to his friend Moussu Laouren. He climbed slowly and cautiously, fearing to find the mother-bird in the nest. This, unfortunately for him, proved to be the case; for as he approached the nest he saw the eagle sitting on her young, to keep them warm, no doubt.

He would gladly have turned around without being seen by the bird but she had seen him and came out of her nest, left her young, jumped on poor Mèsté Règé, fastened her beak onto the back of his neck, her talons onto the seat of his breeches and carried him up in the air.

Mèsté Règé thought himself lost; he prayed God to

receive his soul.   Meanwhile the eagle was soaring higher
and going toward the sea.   When out upon the Mediterranean, the bird said to herself : " Now I had better drop
him, I am far enough from the land, he cannot swim
ashore, he will be drowned so he can never trouble me
again." So saying, she unfastened her talons from Mèsté
Règé's breeches and her beak from the back of his neck ;
she dropped him and returned to her nest.

Poor Mèsté Règé fell into the water from such a height
that he was stunned and lost consciousness.   However
it was only for a little while, for he soon came to and
shouted for help.

Fortunately there was a boat quite near and the crew
hastened to see what the object was.   To their great surprise the sailors saw that it was a man struggling in the
water.   They took him into the boat and plied him with
questions.   Mèsté Règé related his adventures to the
sailors and they believed him at first, sailors are such a
credulous set, but soon a tremendous tempest arose
which threatened to engulf them all.   But if sailors
are credulous they are also superstitious, and they
soon whispered amongst themselves that the cause of
the tempest was, no doubt, the man they had rescued
from drowning.

"God must be displeased with us," they said, "this
man is some evil being whom we should not have fished
out of the sea.   Let us throw him to the mercy of the
waves and perhaps God will be appeased."

Poor Mèsté Règé, hearing their conversation, fell on his knees and said to them: "My dear friends, I am a man like yourselves, I am no evil being or supernatural creature, I have told the truth regarding my whole adventure and how you came to find me here."

But as the wind blew more and more, and the tempest increased in violence, they refused to believe him; they seized him and began to tie him hand and foot before throwing him overboard.

Mèsté Règé seeing himself lost, and knowing that his time had come, and that his end was near, said: "My friends, you have here empty wine-casks; put me inside of one and throw it overboard and perhaps some charitable soul may find me and save me."

What he asked was granted; they put him inside a cask and threw him into the sea.

The sailors had not guessed right, however; the tempest increased in fury, so that the vessel was nearly swamped by huge waves falling repeatedly on deck.

As for Mèsté Règé, he was so much tossed in his cask, and so much bruised against the sides, that he nearly fainted from exhaustion and pain; although praying all the while that God would send some charitable soul to his rescue. He was about to give up hope, not knowing how far out he was, when suddenly the sea, which throws up everything that floats on its surface, by a great billow hove ashore the cask.

Oh! said he; I am no longer in the water. He placed

his eye at the bunghole and looked out. Suddenly he thought he heard the tramp of an animal and, fortunately, he was not mistaken. It was a cow looking for some object against which to scratch her back. She scratched and scratched; the cask turned and turned, Mèsté Règé with it. Bruised as he was, this second shaking suited him not, but it brought the cow's tail against the bunghole; quietly and skillfully he drew it in with his finger, rolled it around his wrist, and held on to it with both hands. As soon as the cow was through rubbing and felt her tail held fast, she set out to run at her best speed. Mèsté Règé was all the while holding on for dear life, saying to himself. "Unless the tail comes off, wherever she goes, I will go, also."

The cow ran, dragging the cask for at least an hour; then, being tired out, she took the road to her master's barn. On entering the yard she turned the corner at such speed that the cask struck the gate post and broke to pieces.

Mèsté Règé, thus liberated, looked about him and said: "Why, this is my own house!" Then he heard cries and lamentations inside and, without waiting a moment to take breath, he rapped at the door, saying: "Open, please." The wife and children in tears, opened the door and let him in.

All fell on his neck, even Moussu Laouren, who had come to console them. Then he related his thrilling adventures; they all thanked God for his miraculous preservation, tears were dried, mourning was changed to joy, and the happy reunion was celebrated by a feast which lasted eight days.

When Mèsté Rinaou had done relating the story, the children thanked him, bade him good night, and went up stairs to bed, to dream, no doubt, of the wonderful adventures of Mèsté Règé. Pretty soon Mèsté Rinaou bade us, also, good-bye. I inquired of my host the age of Mèsté Rinaou. " He is ninety-five years old," said my friend, " and it is a pity you cannot spend a few days with us, and hear a few more stories from him; the old gentleman knows them by the dozen."

Early in the morning, after having partaken of a good breakfast and thanked my kind friends, I proceeded on my way.

The whole forenoon I traveled alone, noticing every blade of grass and weed by the wayside, the trees and birds. " Train your eyes to observe every object you meet, listen to every proper conversation you hear," my father had said to me, " and you will come back to us filled with knowledge of things and men."

About noon, seven or eight men caught up with me. They asked my name, where I was from, and where I was bound for. I answered their questions, and the whole band of us set to walking by twos. The man by my side might have been fifty years old, and, knowing that I was a stranger to that part of the country, he very obligingly answered all my questions about the different villages we passed through and the objects of interest we met. He also volunteered much information about the lords and noted men of the country. I was so much absorbed in what he was saying, that I did not notice we were at the top of a hill. When suddenly he exclaimed:

"Té! Do you see the castle on yonder eminence, surrounded by that park which slopes gently to the banks of the stream? Well, that is the castle of La Ferrière, for years the devil haunted it, and finally was driven off by three powerful men."

My eyes were taking in the castle, which impressed me as a princely residence, and the scenery about it which could not be surpassed ; but, at the mention of the devil, I turned towards my companion, and, seeing his earnestness, I kept back the incredulous smile which was already on my lips. I had never heard of the devil being seen nor of his haunting any place, excepting the hearts of men. My father was not superstitious, and had warned me against such nonsense; but, unwilling to offend the kind old man, I feigned astonishment, and said I had never heard of the devil in a castle, nor of strong men who could put him out, but I would like to know about them. My companion asked for nothing better, and said:

"I am surprised you never heard the story. Everybody in this country knows it as well as I do. It is pretty long, but we have plenty of time."

The Story of the
Three Strong Men,—
Crowbar,
Hookbeard,
and the Miller.

Three Strong Men

IN the village of Vèzénobre a good peasant took for a
wife a woman so stout and strong that she was known
in the village as Marion the Stout. This pair had a
twenty-four month baby, a most remarkable child, and
he became a great man.

At birth, he was like a three-year-old, with full set of
teeth, long hair, strong and shapely limbs, and a splendid
form.

At fifteen, he was as large as a man of thirty, and his
strength was marvelous for his age. He could lift with
one hand a sack of wheat, and he played with an anvil
as a toy.

At the age of twenty, he was as well-formed and as
strong as the Colossus of Rhodes.

His strength became proverbial in the country. All
wrestlers feared him; for none could withstand his
feats in the ring. With one hand he would seize his
opponent and hold him at arm's length for a long time,
then he would whirl him about his head until he cried
"King's truce!" when he would stretch him at full
length on the ground. There was not his equal in the
country.

When he had attained to manhood, he started on a long journey to visit the villages and towns of France. He saw Lyons, Marseilles, Nimes, and was on his way to Bordeaux, traveling on foot, with a big axle-tree for a cane, when he reached the little village of Fontanès. There he took his dinner, visited an old castle belonging to the Lieutenant-General of the King's army, and, at one o'clock, he set out for the village of Lecques, which is perched on a rock on the right bank of the River Le Vidourle.

The owner of the castle of Fontanès was a powerful lord, to whom the villagers owed obedience. He could command them in season and out of season. Was his woodyard empty, a word from his steward brought twenty loads of wood; was his ice-house empty, the peasants were set to work cutting ice on the river and packing it for the summer use of his lordship. During seed-time, they had to turn out with their teams, and plow, harrow, and sow his lordship's broad acres.

When Crowbar reached Fontanès it was seed-time and the peasants were at work sowing the grain in a large field on a cross-road leading to Lecques. Some of the peasants were ploughing, some harrowing, some sowing the grain, some were singing, others swearing at their teams or goading their oxen. Among them was a ploughman with a gray mule as lazy as his master, and following behind was his son, a lad of ten, cracking the whip once in a while on the mule's back.

Old Dumas, for that was the ploughman's name, was singing in a tremulous voice with a Gallic accent:

> I was sitting the oak boughs below,
> I saw bustling toward me my love,
> 'T was Clarissa looking for her beau,
> Took me for him, bounced into my lap.

(Interrupting himself). "Get up Falet! hit him hard, boy."

> If you love me be not proud,
> If you love me why so haughty?
> Time is past to play at scorn,
> When one's promised then 't is naughty.

"Get up, Falet; that hole won't swallow you up; get up!"

Not far behind ploughed another big tall fellow with a beard touching the ground. He was nicknamed Hookbeard on account of his beard turning up at the end. He was a man of extraordinary strength, for he could lift almost any weight which one might tie to his beard.

He was ploughing with a yoke of oxen and was singing the song of the ploughman:

> When the ploughman ends the furrow
> Then he throws aside his ploughshare,
> When the ploughman ends the furrow
> Then he throws aside his ploughshare;
> His ploughshare.
>
> He finds his wife beside the fire,
> Sad and inconsolable.
> He finds his wife beside the fire,
> Sad and inconsolable;
> Sad and inconsolable.

If you are sick, tell me,
  I will make for you a pottage;
If you are sick, tell me,
  I will make for you a pottage;
     A pottage.

A pottage with a cabbage
  And a lean sparrow.
A pottage with a cabbage
  And a lean sparrow;
     A lean sparrow.

If you are dead, say so,
  We will bury you in the wine-vault.
If you are dead, say so,
  We will bury you in the wine-vault;
     In the wine-vault.

Your head under the faucet
  To drink as it flows.
Your head under the faucet
  To drink as it flows;
     To drink as it flows.

As Crowbar appeared at the crossroad, Hookbeard was at the end of the furrow.

"Well, neighbor, the plough must run easy since the ploughman is singing," said Crowbar.

"Well," replied Hookbeard, "sometimes easy, and sometimes hard; but withal time flies. We are working for the lord of the manor; we receive no pay; we need not kill ourselves."

And from one thing to another the talk ran on. Crowbar, meanwhile, was toying with his axle, as one would with a cane. When about to start, he said, swinging his axle as a pointer to show off his strength, "which road goes to Lecques? This one or that?"

Hookbeard's face grew purple as a poppy, and seizing the ploughbeam with one hand, he raised it from the furrow, oxen and all, so that to Crowbar they seemed to fly. He swung them in the air in the right direction, and said:

"Take this road;" and let them down easy in the furrow again.

"Why," said Crowbar, "I should say you have a powerful wrist, my good fellow. I have traveled extensively and seen many strong men; but I have yet to find your equal. If you like," added he: "We will become partners, and together make the tour of France."

"I am willing," replied Hookbeard; "but I have no money, and to travel one needs money."

"Do n't let that hinder you," said Crowbar, "I have enough for both. Besides, we can earn some on the way."

Hookbeard, without further parley, left his oxen in the furrow, and arm-in-arm with Crowbar set out for Lecques.

Lecques is built on a rock on the right bank of the river Le Vidourle.

To reach the village the stream must be crossed by ferry-boat. When the two men reached the left bank of the river, the boat was on the other side, and no ferry-man in sight. They shouted and roared, but nobody heard. It was the hottest part of the day, and no doubt the Lecquars were all asleep.

"What shall we do?" said Crowbar to his companion; "shall we wait here until somebody comes to the river"?

"Not much!" exclaimed the other; "just hang to my whiskers, and you 'll be quickly over."

Crowbar put his axle under his arm, seized his friend's beard with both hands, and with a swing and a jerk, Hookbeard sent him flying over the stream. Crowbar landed on his feet, went to the boat, unfastened it, rowed across the river, and ferried over his friend.

After making the boat fast, they set out towards the gristmill, below the village, in hope of finding somebody.

The miller had just dined, and to work off his dinner,

was playing quoits with his millstones on the sand. When Hookbeard and Crowbar saw the miller, they exclaimed:

"Here is a man as strong as we; let us invite him to join us. All three together we could defy the world."

They approached, and politely complimented the miller on his strength; and, by way of introduction, they each picked up a millstone.

The miller delighted to find his equals, invited them in, treated them to wine, and they talked of their exploits, each making as big a story as possible. When they had drunk and rested enough, Crowbar said to the miller:

"I have traveled much, hoping to find men as strong as I, but have seen none until to-day I met Hookbeard, and he has consented to go with me. Why should you not come too? We three should have nothing to fear. Won't you come?"

The miller was much attached to his mill, and asked time to make up his mind.

"Stay until to-morrow with me," he said; "have a good supper and a night's rest, then I will give you my decision."

An expert at fishing, he soon caught fish enough for supper, and the feast was spread, the best wine brought out, and at the height of the feast the miller anticipated his answer, and agreed to go with them.

Early next morning they took a bite to stay their

stomachs, and were about to start on their journey, when the miller said to his companions :

" I will take my millstones with me; when we have nothing better to do, we can have a game of quoits."

" Quite right," both replied at once; " take them along."

The miller closed his mill, placed the key under the door, took a millstone under each arm, and off they went.

They worked their way towards Montpelier, passed La Fontade, climbed the hill of La Peña, crossed the woods of La Clause, reached St. Beauzeli, and wherever they went they performed feats of strength.

People were surprised to see such powerful men, one with a beard trailing the ground, another with an immense axle-tree for a cane, and a third with millstones in his pockets. Children swarmed about them, and followed them through the streets.

One evening at an inn they were telling of their exploits to the villagers, exaggerating their performances and boasting of their bravery. One of the listeners spoke up, and said :

" If you have the courage you claim, you ought to render me a service."

" What is it ? " said the three, all at once.

" In the loft of my barn, at about two every morning, something runs over the floor, and there is a noise like the dragging of chains. My men pretend that a dragon haunts the barn; they saw him one night, they say, and

after nightfall they cannot be induced to enter the barn, much less to sleep in the loft. If you would spend a night there, find out the cause of alarm and, perhaps, kill the dragon, then my men would attend to their evening chores and sleep in the loft, as they used to do."

The trio replied they would be glad to do as much for him and, proud of the occasion, they set out for the barn.

Crowbar said: "There is no need of three; give my companions a room. I will stay alone in the barn, and will call you if I need help." So the miller and Hook-beard, who had not the courage of Crowbar, were glad to sleep in the house.

When Crowbar was alone he examined every nook of the loft, and the heaps of fodder upon the floor, to make sure that nothing was hidden there. He looked out of the windows, and found that one opened upon the village green, the other looked out upon a neighbor's yard, and was only six feet from the ground, the barn being on sloping ground. This window he could not fasten; it had been always left open for ventilation. Crowbar threw himself upon the straw, but not to sleep. Hardly had an hour passed when he heard a noise at the open window. He raised on one elbow, and listened. The sound approached, as if some creature was walking on the boards with heavy nailed shoes or hard hoofs, he could not tell which. At the same time there was the clank, clank, of a chain dragged by jerks on the floor. It came still nearer, and Crowbar sprang towards it with a shout.

"So, dragon, here you are, hey! Oust me from this barn, if you can!"

The object turned, and went tearing through the barn, Crowbar after it. The chase began; the racket roused the village, the two climbed the haymow, and leaped from one stack to another; they vaulted over each other, and fell in a heap on the floor; they sprang up and clattered like mad through the barn again. The noise was terrific,— it lasted twenty minutes. At last, by mere luck, Crowbar stepped on the chain, stooping, he quickly seized it, and, with a powerful jerk, he got the creature within grasp. He laid firm hold of it with both arms, muttering to himself:

"Dragon though ye be, down with ye!" and he flung it out the window on to the village green.

The peasants, who were outside listening to the racket, rushed in, and found Crowbar in a dripping sweat.

"I do not know what sort of beast it is," said he, "but it has led me a chase, I can assure you."

"Let us see what it is," and they rushed out into the square, and found,— you cannot guess,— a goat! A goat burst asunder by the fall!

And this is its story: The owner of the goat had no fodder, so every night he let the goat loose. She, with a bound, leaped into the neighbor's loft, by the open window, and fed all night on the hay

Evil-doers are often caught in their own traps.   If the man had not left the chain on the goat, to make the frightful clatter, he might not have been betrayed.

Next morning, when the story spread abroad in the village, everybody said that is just like him, shiftless fellow; that is one of his old tricks.   And, from that day, none of them would have anything to do with the unfortunate loser of the goat.

The owner of the barn, well pleased with the outcome of the adventure, entertained the three strong men royally.   He gave a public feast in their honor, and, in the presence of all the dignitaries of the village, he thanked them for their services, and, from that time on, he kept his barn-door and windows locked.

Meanwhile, the fame of the three strong men was ever widening.

Farther up the mountain lived a rich gentleman in an old castle.   He had been a merchant, had amassed a fortune in commerce, and wishing to retire with his family, had bought the castle with large estates, and had it repaired and fitted up to his taste.

On the first floor was drawing-room, boudoirs, dining-room, and kitchen.   The sleeping-rooms of the family were on the second floor, and the third floor was given up to the servants.

Almost all the windows had gratings.   The tower, or ancient keep, on the western corner of the castle, was left unrepaired, as it was not needed.   The doors had the old rusty locks, and the windows were not fastened at all, excepting in stormy weather.

On the second floor, between the master's room and the tower, was a room daintily furnished and prepared for the daughter when she should come home from her convent.

At the castle nothing was lacking. There were carriages of all sorts; equipages on equipages; servants on servants; horses of all breeds, for the carriage and for the saddle. Besides there were two immense New Foundland dogs, named Sultan and Mustafa. Sultan was fat and black, and Mustafa was lean and red. They were tied by day and loosed by night.

When the merchant came to live on his domain early in May, the country was beautiful to see. The trees were in full bloom, and the meadows a magnificent green. Half way up the Cevennes, they had the mountain air first hand; it was neither hot nor cold, and too far from the marshes for mosquitoes.

The gentleman was all delight with his new possessions, and nothing was lacking but the presence of his daughter.

So he looked forward to her vacation when she should come and regain strength and spirits in the pleasures of outdoor life at the castle. And you should have seen the reception they gave her the day she came.

The whole household was on foot to receive her, but none welcomed her more warmly than the old bonne

Jeaneton, who had brought her up since her mother died in childhood. Her first evening at the castle was one of festivity. Joy and happiness were seen on all faces.

Bedtime came, they all wished the young mistress good night, and Jeaneton took her to her beautiful chamber, the furniture and appointments of which were fit for a queen. The dogs were let loose, the doors closed, the lights put out, and all about the castle was soon silent and dark. The young Miss was soon asleep, so were the others of the household.

About midnight the girl felt something pressing on her feet. She thought she was dreaming. But no; she was not dreaming. Something heavy and warm was on her feet. She heard it breathing. Fear seized her. Had she cried, her father in the next room would have come to her rescue. But no ; she kept still, covered her head with the sheet, and stayed thus without stirring the whole night. It was enough to frighten one to death, but when one's time has not come, it takes more than that to kill one.

A little before daybreak, she felt something rise, heard it jump from the bed, and leave the room quietly. You may well imagine how impatient she was for daylight to come.

At breakfast she appeared pale, distracted, with black rings under her eyes, telling the tale of a sleepless night.

"What is the matter with you, my child," inquired her father, "have you not slept well?"

She fell on his neck, and with tears in her eyes, told him of her great fright. Her father, much surprised and greatly pained, said to her: "My child do not divulge this to any one, I shall find means to discover the cause of your fright; and if the servants heard of this not one of them would stay at the castle."

They kept it secret, and under a pretext, induced old Jeaneton to occupy the room. The first night the old nurse slept in the beautiful chamber, the master took pains himself to lock the doors and windows, and even fastened the windows of the old tower.

The next morning father and daughter were dying to know how she spent the night.

"Oh! I slept as sound as a top," said she; "why should I not, in so fine a room and such a soft bed?"

For some time the master attended to closing the doors and windows himself; but, at length, as nothing disturbed old Jeaneton, he grew careless, and left the tower window open.

One early morning Jeaneton rushed into her young mistress' room quaking with terror, and told her that a strange animal had lain on her feet during the night; she had heard it breathing heavily, but it had left before dawn, and she could not tell what it was.

The father was notified, and again, on account of the servants, they all agreed to keep the affair secret.

About this time the fame of the Three Strong Men reached them, and the owner of the castle set out to fetch them. He brought them to his house as guests. Crowbar offered to occupy the room, but Hookbeard insisted that it was his turn, pompously adding: "If die I must, ready I am." So it was decided for him to have the first chance at the beast. The servants were, to be sure, surprised to see a man with such a beard about to sleep in the dainty bed of the young mistress, but they kept their comments to themselves.

Hookbeard spread himself out on the pretty bed, and thought:

"Ghost or devil that haunts this room, I admire your taste; you have not badly chosen your couch."

Wiser, however, than the nurse and her mistress, he did not go to sleep.

At the moment of expectation, he heard a sound like an animal moving in the room and scenting. He stretched his hand, felt a cold nose, a head, a tongue that licked his hand.

"If all the ghosts, devils, and dragons are no worse than this one," thought Hookbeard, "they are not to be feared." And, patting the animal, they became friends; so much so, that they spent the night together, the beast with its head in Hookbeard's arms.

What a surprise to the master it was when he came into the room in the morning to find the long-bearded fellow stretched out, and in his arms the head of the dog, Mustafa.

Quickly he brought his daughter and Jeaneton to see the devil of their midnight terror.

How could the dog have got in?

Leaning against the old tower, just below one of its windows, was a low shed. At night, when the dogs were let loose, Mustafa found nothing easier than to jump on the roof of the shed, from thence through the tower window, and from the tower into the young lady's room.

It is not known whether Mustafa dreaded the night's dew on account of rheumatism, but evidently he preferred to sleep on a soft bed to spending his night under the beautiful stars in the court.

Overjoyed, the owner of the castle complimented Hookbeard for his bravery, gave the Three Strong Men a handsome reward, entertained them two or three days, and, on taking leave of them, said:

"I have a friend who lives not far from Alais, in the castle of La Ferrière; I believe he needs you."

"Let us go at once," said the three; "what can he need us for?"

"He will tell you," replied the gentleman; "tell him I have sent you."

Thereupon they set out, with paunches and pockets full, a jolly set of rovers. They walked for many days and, finally, about ten o'clock in the morning of a fine

October day, they reached the lodge of La Ferrière. They sounded the knocker, and presented their request to meet the master of the castle. The servant, in a great state of alarm, rushed in upon the master while he was shaving, with the news that three tremendous fellows, the sight of which was enough to frighten any one, were waiting in the office to see him. One carried an axle-tree as a cane, another had a mill-stone in each coat pocket, and the third wore a beard that touched the ground and turned up at the end ; they were three veritable Samsons.

"What do they want?" said the Marquis.

"On my word I do not know; they only asked to speak with you."

"I will be down presently; tell them to wait." One moment later the Marquis entered his office and was surprised, in spite of his warning, to see such powerful looking fellows.

Our three men bowed respectfully, told of their adventures at the castle in the Cevennes, and offered to rid the Marquis of any beast or devil that might disturb his peace.

"I will give you a great reward," replied the Marquis, "if you can rid me of an enemy that has long damaged my place, and especially is the cause of my wife and children remaining away from the castle."

"I cannot keep a servant here except this old man

who has positively refused to leave me in spite of the
evil reports."

" It is said in the neighborhood that the devil haunts
my castle and everybody keeps away from it."

" I do not know the cause, but, from time to time I
miss some chickens, rabbits, turkeys and geese; even
once I lost an ox.   We have searched again and again,
but without results.   I have watched day and night and
never have seen a stray man or beast on the premises,
yet, when least expecting it, something is stolen.   Some
of the servants have been badly beaten when alone;
taken unawares, struck from behind, but even they have
never seen the enemy."

" This is why I can keep no one at my castle and they
say it is the devil's abode.   Now, if you can find out
what all this means, you will render a great service to
me and the community."

" Be no longer uneasy," they said, " we shall unravel
the mystery and that right soon.   Make us acquainted
with every nook of your castle, your garden, your park,
and then we will tell you how we intend to proceed."

The Marquis first invited them to dine.   After dinner
he took them through the castle from cellar to garret and
over the garden and park even to a clump of trees beyond the park.   The Marquis meanwhile was giving
them all kinds of information, but the three said not a
word.   Silently they surveyed the ground, scrutinized
the nooks and corners, peering into the shrubbery, rak-

ing among the heaps of dead leaves and striking the ground in search of pitfalls.

When the search was over they proposed to the Marquis that they be left alone in charge of the castle to follow their own line of action. The Marquis agreed and accordingly prepared to leave the estate in their charge with abundant supplies at their disposal, and he and the old servant left next morning.

Crowbar and his friends took a walk in the afternoon, looked about everywhere, but saw nothing suspicious. The following day they laid a plan to station themselves as spies to watch every avenue leading to the castle and they watched all day in vain. The next day was the same without results. This was growing monotonous; they became bolder and said: "The devil must be afraid of us; he dares not show himself. This will turn out like other devil stories; the fox has eaten the hens, the wolf eaten the ox — you will see — nevertheless if it be the devil let him show himself, we will fix him."

Thus, tired of suspense, they decided that two of them should go hunting and the third should keep watch on the premises, just to be on the safe side, not that they expected to see anything or anybody.

This time the miller said: "It is my turn; I will stay and if the devil comes, I will make a pancake of him with my millstones."

"Remain," said the other two; "each one his turn, nothing is more just." Crowbar and Hookbeard started for the chase at day-break, their guns on their shoulders like true poachers. They went through the park, passed by the clump of trees, crossed a small stream and went on to the mountains. They were in luck, they killed much game and returned with their bags full.

As soon as his companions were gone, the miller placed himself on the watch but as before saw nothing. Then he set about preparing dinner for his friends. What he cooked for the meal I do not remember, perhaps they never told me or I may have forgotten it, but that can be of no great consequence.

About eleven o'clock he set the table and had things ready so as not to keep them waiting on their return, then he sat down before the door saying to himself: "As soon as I see them coming I will pour out the pottage." He waited a long while, his comrades did not show up; it was very hot; sleep overtook him and he fell nodding.

The devil, who was lurking unseen, stealthily approached the table, took the tablecloth by the four corners with all its contents, spoons, forks, dishes, bottles, glasses, etc., clubbed the miller on his way out and left him senseless.

A little while after, the hunters came, and what did they see?

The poor miller stretched on the ground, his face all bloody, more dead than alive. Quickly they fetched some vinegar, made him smell it, washed his face with it, and made him drink a glass of Riquiqui, placed him in an arm-chair, rubbed him with *Eau Sedative*, and, little by little, he came to, but he could not tell what had happened. He had neither heard nor seen anything, so that the trio were none the wiser for the miller's mishap. For some time, however, they redoubled their vigils, but with no luck.

Meanwhile, the miller recovered, and, when himself again, Hookbeard broke out one evening at table with "Well, friends, go hunting to-morrow. I shall stay here. We must find out what all this means. I will try my best not to be surprised; and, if I can only see him, whether man, beast, or devil, he won't leave this place scot free."

The next day the miller and Crowbar went hunting, promising to return early.

Hookbeard made all his preparations,—killed a fowl for a roast, made an omelette for entremet, a rabbit stew for entrée, a purée of peas for pottage, and fritters of squash for dessert. He set the table early; then he walked about the room, with his hands behind him and with a look of satisfaction and scorn upon his face, as if nothing could happen to him. He paced the room for one hour, for two hours; finally got tired, and, to his misfortune, sat down.

Sleep is so treacherous that it overcame him. No sooner had he closed his eyes and begun to nod, than he was clubbed on the head, and so completely stunned that he gave no signs of life when his two friends came. They thought him dead, but did all they could to revive him, and at last succeeded.

He was a long time recovering. It took the good care of his two comrades, a long rest, and good food to restore him to health.

When Hookbeard was on his feet again, Crowbar said:

"My friends, both of you have had your thrashing. We cannot leave here without my getting one. If I have to leave my skin in the attempt, I must know who is haunting this place. To-morrow leave me alone in the castle and go hunting."

They obeyed; but before setting out Hookbeard said to Crowbar:

"Don't go to sleep; don't sit down. Sleep is a rascal which overcomes the most wary. If you are caught napping, as the miller and I have been, you run the risk of getting a drubbing you will never forget."

"Thanks," replied Crowbar; "I will do my best to keep awake."

When alone, he set out to get dinner. It was not at all elaborate, and was soon ready. Before ten o'clock his table was set, and he was pacing the floor, as Hookbeard had done. Then he sat down; soon his head was bobbing up and down, falling from one shoulder to the other, as if fast asleep. Through his half-closed eyes, however, he was watching the room and the park.

Pretty soon he spied in the garden something black,

which seemed to be moving behind the trees. Nodding all the more, as if fast asleep, Crowbar saw the black object advancing cautiously from tree to tree, and bush to bush, but so quick in its movements that he could hardly make out its shape; its general appearance was like this:

A black body, flat face, large, round, yellowish eyes, which shone like a cat's in the dark, two horns, short and sharp, a long tail, curled up to its shoulders, thin legs, and long hands, with fingers like a griffin's, and it was not more than three feet high.

Crowbar understood that it was the very devil that was the fear of the neighborhood.

Before he sat down he had been careful to place his axle-tree within reach. Thus prepared, he awaited the approach.

The devil, no doubt, believed him asleep, approached noiselessly, entered the room, went to the table, and reached for the table-cloth. Crowbar sprang to his feet, and struck at him. The devil, ever on the alert, had seen Crowbar's motion, and turned to leap out of the window. It was lucky for him that he turned round when he did. He was too far to be hit on the head, but received a blow between the shoulders from Crowbar's axle-tree, that sent him sprawling in the yard.

Nimbly he turned a somersault, was on his feet in a flash, and made for the park. Crowbar gave chase. The devil fairly flew, with Crowbar close behind. They

ran from alley to alley, from avenue to avenue; they
went through the park, and round and round it. No
doubt, the devil, seeing his pursuer to be such a big
fellow, thought to tire him out, leave him behind,
find his hole, and disappear; but Crowbar gained on
him, and struck him several times between the shoulder-
blades with his axle-tree; so the devil thought best to
seek his hole, even at the risk of revealing his hiding-
place.

Running then to the clump of trees, under a wild
laurel, he lifted a large, flat stone, and disappeared from
under the very nose of Crowbar, at the very moment he
thought he had him.

Crowbar examined the hole, replaced the stone, put
his cane over it to hold it down, and returned to the
castle, sweating like a leper, from his run.

The hunters were already there. As they did not see
him, they said he must be dead.

" Indeed," said the miller, " the devil struck me once;
you got a first-rate thrashing; no doubt, he has killed
Crowbar."

They feigned the greatest distress; they rang all the
bells; they called; they searched every nook in the castle
— no one.

Hookbeard was thoughtful and silent. The miller,
who seemed the most eager to hunt him up, was saying
to himself:

" He got his thrashing like us. He will know now what

the devil is like. He was telling us that we should leave our skins rather than get away from here without unraveling this mystery. Well, if the devil has skinned him, so much the worse for him. At any rate, he will no longer poke fun at us."

Just as he was saying this to himself, Crowbar arrived, mopping his brow with his handkerchief, and said to them:

"I made it hot for him. He escaped me by a miracle. I watched him coming until he reached the table, and, had he not turned round and jumped, I should have killed him on the spot. As it was, I gave him a hot chase, but he made me run, I tell you! Do you know where he went down? Well, I will show you."

And he related to them how it all had happened, how he had feigned sleep, had spied him behind a tree, what his size was, how his head and eyes looked, his horns, his legs and hands, and all about him. He took them to the clump of trees, removed the axle-tree and the stone; they decided to go down the hole, with the help of pulleys and ropes, find the devil's hiding-place, and settle him for good.

The day following, they fixed a windlass at the opening of the cave. They bought three or four miles of rope, and made all kinds of preparations to carry out their scheme. This busied them all day, and, as prudence required them to make the descent by daylight, they postponed operations until the next day.

In the evening, at table, the miller, jealous of Crowbar's achievement, and coveting the honor of killing the devil, said that he would go down first; that he would do this and that; he would smash the devil to a pancake with one blow of his millstones.

"We cannot all go at once," said the other two. "If you wish to go first, we give you the precedence."

At early dawn the next day, the trio went to the hole. Tying a strong basket to the rope, the miller sat in it, with millstones in his pockets, and gave the signal to be lowered.

Crowbar and Hookbeard began to unwind the rope, and the miller was lowered into the hole.

So long as he looked up and saw the light, all went well, but when he looked down he became dizzy. Besides, you know that a rope will get all twisted in winding up, and when unwound, the weight attached to it will whirl and whirl. This is precisely what happened when the miller sat in the basket. His weight held the rope taut, and the twists gave the basket a whirling motion. The deeper he went the faster turned the rope. He held to the rope with all his might, but the whirling made him sick, and he was in a sad plight. At last, getting scared, he said to himself:

"How stupid men are at times! For a little honor, why should I leave my bones in this hole? Let the devil go to the deuce! If the other two want to die, let them die!" And, gathering all his strength in his voice, he shouted: "Pull me up! Pull me up!"

He was pulled up. When he reached the opening his face was like wax. They quickly gave him a drop to settle his stomach. Then Hookbeard said, coolly:

"You got scared, miller. I'll take your place, and I believe I shall have a little more courage."

And he sat in the basket. The miller said to him:

"You should take a stick, or something, to defend yourself; you go with your arms hanging, as if you were going to a fête. You don't know what awaits you."

Hookbeard replied: "I don't need anything. Let me put my paws on him, and he is done for. I will split him in two, as I would an acorn."

While saying this, his face grew purple with anger, and his eyes shot fire, and his hands were clinched, as if he meant what he said. Whether he was angry with the miller for coming up is not certain, but he was awfully agitated.

Finally the windlass began turning, and he was slowly lowered into the hole.

No doubt the temperature below was cooler than above ground. So, little by little, Hookbeard's blood cooled and his fury calmed, for he soon felt chills creeping over him; his feet grew cold, and he was in need of a cordial to keep up his courage. He had already gone deeper than the miller, when an idea struck him.

"If we should build a wall over the hole," thought

he, "the devil could not come out again, and without any risk we should win our reward. Let me suggest this to my companions," and with two powerful lungs he shouted: "Pull me up! Pull me up!"

They pulled him up. The miller longed to tease him, and was glad he had been no braver than he. As soon as Hookbeard showed his head he began:

"Ha! ha! You thought I was scared! And you— what have you had? A fright, I suppose. Why did you turn round?"

"I afraid?" roared Hookbeard; "I afraid? You do not know me. An idea struck me, and I wished to make you share it ; but I am ready to go down again."

"What is your idea?" asked Crowbar.

"See," replied Hookbeard, "if we should build a vault a little way down the hole, and pile in stones to the level of the ground, the devil could not get out, and without much trouble and no risk, we should have earned our reward."

"Right you are," said the miller. "Let us do it; let us do it!"

"No!" retorted Crowbar; "you would make fun of me, and if it be only to go a little farther than Hookbeard, I will try it."

So saying, he removed the basket, tied his axle to the rope, sat astride it, and gave the word to be lowered.

In his turn, Crowbar was turning in space. Cool as a cucumber, however, he lighted his pipe, and, when too far down to see, he took a candle from his pocket, lighted it, and went still lower.

His companions knew by the rope that he had gone lower than they, and they expected to hear at any moment his shout to be hoisted up.

But no, nothing; the more rope they gave the deeper he went. Finally, when the rope was about all spent, they heard that he had reached bottom.

Crowbar untied his cane, and by his candle-light saw that he was far from being out of the cave. He walked and walked, not knowing whether he was under the Alps, or the Pyrennees, in Tyrol, or Andalusia. When he saw daylight, he found himself in a magnificent lodge, built of the fine stones of La Clote, in all the perfection of high art.

Surprised, he said to himself: " This surely cannot be the devil's abode, it is too fine."

He went out, and found himself on the edge of a splendid park, in a beautiful country. There were large meadows, watered by canals of pure water; there were fine avenues and stately trees, and far in the park he could see a lordly castle.

More and more surprised, he advanced, cane in hand, seeing no one, but seen of the devil, whose sharp eyes saw from afar.

Sneaking to his castle, chattering: " Oh, the scoundrel! here he is! My gracious, I am lost!" the devil shut himself in his room, shaking like an aspen-leaf.

His back still hurt him from the blow received two days before from Crowbar's cane.

Crowbar went on to the castle, trusting in his strength, but keeping a sharp lookout, for he knew the devil to be treacherous. He reached the gate and knocked—no one appeared; he walked to the entrance door, and pulled the knocker—no one came. He then opened the door, and found himself in a large room sumptuously furnished. Finding nobody there, he opened another door, and found himself in the presence of a young and charming lady, to whom he made a most profound bow.

She motioned him to keep still, and pointed to another door, letting him understand that there was the devil's room.

Quick as a flash, Crowbar, with a blow from his cane, broke the door open and made a rush for the devil, who, nimble as a cat, leaped from the window. Crowbar jumped after him, and then took place on the grounds the liveliest race ever seen.

Every time the devil got within reach, Crowbar prodded him with his cane, but at every blow the devil increased his gait. They chased each other for more than two hours. At last, Crowbar gaining on the devil, lifted his cane to strike a deadly blow. With a supreme effort, the cane came down, but not on the devil. He had dodged the blow at the turning of an alley, and sprang for the cane, that had fallen from Crowbar's hand in the exertion. Just as he was about to grasp it,

Crowbar leaped on him, and a hand-to-hand fight took place.

Oh! that was a desperate struggle — terrific and horrible to see! The devil shrieked and howled; he scratched and bit; while Crowbar, dumb and purple in the face, gave telling blows with his fists. He could not strike the devil's head, because of the horns, and he could not grab his body, because it was so sleek and slimy. At last the devil's strength gave out. Crowbar seized him by the throat, threw him on his back, put a knee on his breast, and, with the cane in his right hand, gave him a blow between the horns that split his head in two. But he died hard. His head was split open, yet he was struggling, whipping the ground with his tail, and foaming at the mouth. When at last he was still, Crowbar returned to the castle to see to the young lady, whose presence in such a place had so much puzzled him.

She had been the sole witness of the grand fight, and a most interested spectator, for she understood that in Crowbar, if victorious, she would find a deliverer.

So soon as Crowbar appeared in the yard, she hastened to meet him, took him by the hands, and said to him:

"No doubt my father sent you to my rescue. Who are you, and whence are you come? How have you found your way to this spot?

"I have been here for the last three years. How I got here I do not know. I am the king's daughter. I was stolen by that scoundrel you have killed. One day, when I was with my governess on the banks of La Loire, he showed himself suddenly to me, and my fright was so great that I fainted, and when I came to myself again I was in this palace, alone with the arch-fiend. For the last three years he has persecuted me to marry him.

"I cannot tell you all I have suffered, although he was invariably kind and considerate. He gave me all his fancy suggested.

"The villain was always at home nights, but early in the morning he would depart, to be gone all day, and return loaded with plunder in the evening.

"You have no idea of all this castle contains of stolen goods. I will visit the different rooms with you. But first tell me who you are, whence you come, and whether you can deliver me from my prison."

Crowbar briefly told his story, and then, in company with the young princess, visited the castle.

The long corridors were filled with sculpture and paintings, the ceilings were frescoed, the rooms had most magnificent hangings and were furnished with rare and costly furniture. The cellars were full of boxes of all sizes and dimensions, which being opened were found to contain crown jewels and diamonds, silver and gold. Some boxes were full of stolen watches, others held silver spoons and forks, and still others contained precious stones.

The yards about the castle were supplied with fowls

of all kinds, cattle and horses of every breed filled his stables, deer stalked about the park, and pheasants were plenty in the preserve.

When Crowbar had seen everything with his fair guide, he took her to the entrance to the hole through which he had come down, and calling to the miller and Hookbeard, told them to make ready to receive the king's daughter, whom the devil had carried to this lair.

The rope was promptly lowered, an arm-chair, which Crowbar fetched, made fast to it, and the princess sat therein. He securely tied her about the waist, to prevent her falling, and gave the order to hoist her up.

Crowbar staid near until he was sure she had safely reached the top; then he went to fetch all the boxes of jewels and silver and gold.

Hookbeard and the miller received the young lady with all the respect due to her rank. They took her to the castle of La Ferrière, gave her the best room they found, and sent her next day posthaste to her father, the King of France. They then returned to the hole to hear further from Crowbar.

When the princess reached Paris, the king and courtiers, apprised by courier of the miraculous deliverance, went to escort her into the capital. The meeting between the king and his daughter was very affecting. They fell on each other's necks and wept for joy; the whole court, out of sympathy, did likewise.

The first emotion over, the king, full of gratitude toward his daughter's rescuer, remembered his promise made soon after her disappearance.

It should be said that some three years before the young princess was promenading on the banks of the Loire. She dismissed her attendant with the order to come for her at sundown. When the maid came the princess was nowhere to be found. They searched the woods near by, they dragged the river, they scoured the whole country round and made inquiries far and near, but found no trace of her. She had vanished from sight, and nobody could account for her disappearance.

It was then that, in despair, the king issued a proclamation that gave his daughter in marriage to any man who should bring her back.

Hookbeard was the first to hear that the king's daughter was to be the wife of her rescuer.

Good-natured and generous, he said to himself: "What a good thing for Crowbar!" and already became jubilant at the thought of the grand wedding to which he would be invited.

The miller, on the other hand, was jealous and grasping, he said to himself: "Why, I would not refuse her for my wife! If I had not been so afraid, and had gone down the hole, she would now be my bride."

However, each kept his thoughts to himself and both worked away hoisting the boxes which were filled with

diamonds, pearls, rings and bracelets, all sorts of jewels, and plenty of gold and silver.

On seeing this heap of riches at his feet, the miller lost his head, and ventured to say to Hookbeard:

"Now then, for whom have we been working all this time? For Crowbar, no doubt. He very likely will take all this, marry the king's daughter, and we poor fellows, who have helped so much, will get left. If you'll believe me, we will scoop this pile of riches, pull up the rope, and make off."

Hookbeard, kind-hearted but weak, yielded to the miller's reasons. Indeed, the sight of so much gold was enough to lead any man astray. So when Crowbar hallooed, "Hoist me up! There is nothing more to haul up," the miller and Hookbeard removed the windlass, threw the rope in a stream near by, took with them all the treasures, and decamped.

Happily for Crowbar they did not think to cover up the hole, or he would surely have been lost.

In vain did Crowbar call, shout, halloo — nobody replied. He soon guessed the cause of that silence on the part of his friends, and being somewhat of a philosopher, he thought in this wise:

"How mean is human nature! God must have used very dirty clay when He made man. The proverb says that everything God does He does well. Without doubting the truth of the proverb, it seems to me had He used cleaner clay in the making, men would be better than they are."

Not being easily disheartened, Crowbar returned to the castle, saying to himself:

" We shall see later; sometimes the wicked are caught in their own traps."

We have already seen that the king, soon after recovering his daughter, remembered his promise to give her to her rescuer; but as he was a kind father, and very considerate of his daughter's feelings, he spoke to her in this wise:

" In my great despair, and hoping that the offer of your hand to the man who should bring you back might cause my subjects to diligently search for you, I made that promise, and pledged my royal word. Now, I should be very sorry to impose on you a husband who should not be to your liking. Tell me if your rescuer would be acceptable to you, and if I may renew my royal pledge."

"Perfectly acceptable," answered the princess; and thereupon she related to the king all that which took place in the devil's lair, her meeting with Crowbar, his kindness to her, the way he had sent her up the hole, and she added: " I am sure he will please you. He is tall, well-proportioned, handsome, as strong as ten men, and exceedingly kind."

Then the king replied: " Let us await his coming."

And they waited one, two, five months — a year, two

years,—and Crowbar not appearing, the king and his daughter were in despair. What had happened to him? They could not imagine. They tried to hunt up the miller and Hookbeard, but they were not to be found. Whether they had gone to Brussels, St. Petersburg, Egypt, or India, nobody knew.

All this time Crowbar was planning a way of escape from his prison.

Alone in the devil's domain, he roamed through the garden, the park, the woods, the meadows, to find a road leading out of the solitary place. On all sides he found perpendicular walls which no one could think of scaling. Another man would have been discouraged—not Crowbar. He kept saying to himself: "We shall see; we shall see."

One morning, as he lay awake in his bed, the thought came to him that an eagle might perhaps help him out of his predicament. In truth, an eagle was strong enough to bear him up, if it could only be made to do it. He had seen an eagle's nest a day or two before, and he had thought: "If I can tame the mother, I may train the eaglets to do my bidding." So every day he bought meat and put it near the nest. Soon eagle and eaglets were tame enough to eat off his hand. When large enough to leave the nest, the eaglets would follow him around like puppies. As they grew larger they played with him like children. They played hide-and-seek; they climbed on his back; they perched on his shoulders. All the time he fed them the pick of the poultry-yard. Eaglets became eagles, and he tried to teach them to fly with him on their backs; but so strong and heavy was Crowbar, it took two years before one of them could fly any distance with him on its back.

Satisfied at last that the strongest of the lot could sustain his weight for a long flight, he took the bird to the mouth of the hole and, pointing upward, said to the eagle: "Take me up there." And sitting astride on the eagle's wings, they began to ascend. To mount in a straight line being impossible, the eagle whirled round and round the hole until it reached the top. Both rested a while, and then Crowbar caressed the eagle, bade it good-by, and left it to return at leisure.

Crowbar's first inquiry was for his comrades and for the young lady.

He learned that she had gone to Paris, and resided with her father, the king. As for Hookbeard and the miller, they were gone no one knew where. His anxiety was for the lady, however, since it occurred to him that, to hide their conduct, his two companions might have killed her.

Feeling relieved as to her fate, he took a fast horse to Paris, expecting that the king would pay him handsomely for rescuing his daughter. He was not posted as to the king's intentions towards him, and was far from expecting what awaited him in Paris.

Ah! as soon as he presented himself at the palace,

he saw the young princess running down the stairs to greet him. He, somewhat abashed, bowed two or three times, hesitating to enter the palace; but she took him by the hand and led him to her father.

It is needless to describe the reception the king gave him, or the brave man's joy on learning that he was to be the husband of the princess, nor the grand wedding repast given on the marriage day.

As to Hookbeard and the miller, on leaving France, they sold their jewels and precious stones, and deposited the money in a bank. For a while they lived like princes; but one day the bank failed, all depositors lost their money, and the miller and Hookbeard had to beg for a living. They led a miserable existence, sleeping outdoors or in barns in all kinds of weather. This was the harder to bear after their experience of luxury; so one night, as they were out under a tree during a storm, Hookbeard said to the miller:

"We were very wrong to act as we did towards Crowbar; we could have lived just as well on a little less, if we had not have taken the plunder from the devil's lair, and now we should have a friend in Crowbar, who they say, got out of the hole, married the king's daughter, and is now a powerful prince. Now, who dares to go and see him and ask for his help?"

The miller hung his head and made no reply. He felt the more guilty of the two, for it was he who had won over Hookbeard to his plan of abandoning Crowbar.

Nothing further was said that night, and for some time they roughed it as best they could. At last, they could endure that life no longer, and decided to go in search of Crowbar. They would beg his pardon on their knees, and perhaps in his kindness of heart he would forgive them and render some assistance.

Having taken that resolution, they set out for the king's palace. On reaching it they inquired for Crowbar. He came to meet them, and was greatly surprised to see their poverty. His first impulse was to forgive them and treat them kindly; but the king, who knew of their doings, forbade him to receive them, and ordered them thrown into prison, and there they ended their days.

Crowbar, meanwhile, had become a powerful prince, and was much beloved by the king. He reared a large family of children, and finally died in peace and plenty surrounded by many friends.

The castle of La Ferrière became again habitable, since the devil had ceased to haunt it, and the Marquis, his children, and their descendants have dwelt happily in it ever since.

❧   ❧

The Hautboy Player
of Ventabren.

❧   ❧

The Hautboy Player of Ventabrén

WHILE my companion was relating the story of The Three Strong Men, we traveled over considerable ground. The sun was setting when he finished, and we were nearing a town. Several of our fellow-travelers had dropped off by the way, my companion and I shook hands at the gate of the town, and I was left alone to go to the inn.

I spent a very good night there, and the next day I hardly know where I went. I believe that was the day I met the hautboy player — he was a jolly fellow, though! He made it lively for us going through the big woods. I 'll tell you about the hautboy player of Ventabrén.

I had been walking alone through a flat country until, just as I came to an extensive piece of woods, I met a man; and we were going through the woods in company when it happened that, as another trail met ours, we fell in with a man and a small boy.

"Halloa! you here, Fougasse?" shouted my companion, as the man joined us.

"I am he," replied the newcomer.

"Where do you come from?"

"Té! I come from the fête of Garigues."

I took him for a hautboy player. He wore a pigeon feather in his hat, and an unmounted hautboy could be seen sticking out of the pocket of his half-buttoned vest. He carried a bundle swung on the end of a stick over his shoulder — it was a big fougasse tied in a napkin. The little boy carried on his back, strapped to his shoulders, a tambourin, and — *pecaïre!** he could hardly walk with his load, so young was he.

Speaking to the hautboy player, my companion very familiarly called him "Fougasse," and I made bold to say: "But that is not your name."

"Ho! no, indeed; my name is Saouché. Fougasse is my nickname."

"And don't you hate to be called Fougasse?"

"Hate it? no; I would not be a hautboy player if I did — all the hautboy players are nicknamed. It is part of our calling, you know.

"You want to know why I am called Fougasse?

"Well, I was returning from the fête of Garigues, as I am now — this was many years ago. I carried, as now, a fougasse on the end of my stick. The sun was low as we reached this very spot, and we were quietly jogging along, as we are now, when the little fellow with me,

* Poor me!

E.C. PEIXOTTO · 1896 ·

like this one, said: 'Uncle, see that big dog coming behind us.'

"I turned and saw a tremendous wolf ten paces from us. I took two or three steps towards him to frighten him. He stopped, eyed me, and started when I started. I stopped again — he stopped; I walked, and he walked. The night was coming on. I began to get scared. The boy was holding tight to my hand, and we were stretching our legs to the utmost, when the idea struck me that he might be hungry. I would give him a piece of my fougasse, and he would go off to eat it.

"Zoù! I cut a piece, threw it at him, and ran. He made but a mouthful of it. You would think he had not eaten for three days. He showed wicked, sharp, white teeth, which set me thinking; and hardly had he swallowed the fougasse than he followed us again, this time a little closer. I cut him another piece. Zoù! He swallowed it down — quick, too; and little by little the fougasse went. What was to be done? I was at my wits' end. The night was dark; his eyes shone like two lanterns. Directly there were four instead of two piercing me with their wicked glare. Whether it was due to the terrible fright, I am ashamed to own it; but I was sure there were two wolves following us. My hair stood up like the bristles on a hog's back — my hat did not touch my head. Good gracious! I thought to myself, if I had only some more fougasse! I was in a terrible fix.

"We stopped, both of us petrified in our shoes, and

the idea flashed to my mind: 'Perhaps they might like to dance.'

" As quickly as my shaking fingers would let me, I mounted my hautboy and began to play a medley of — I don't know what. The effect was like magic. They stopped, hesitated a moment, and off they went as if the devil was after them. I assure you they did not stop to keep time to the hautboy.

"Did I stop playing? Not I! I played nearly the whole night, until I reached my house. My wife, who was still up, heard the hautboy, and came out on the steps with a light.

"'What do you mean by playing so late in the night? Have you gone crazy?' said she. I told her my adventures. She burst out laughing, and yet laughs every time she thinks of it. Since then I have met many wolves, but I never lose my wits. To one I play a little farandole, to another the waltz of Sardan, and the thing works like a charm — they are off at the first note, and I have no more trouble with them.

" The day after my scare, my wife, who likes gossip, told one of our neighbors confidentially about it; she, of course, told another, and the news spread. Soon I was known as ' La Fougasse.'

"At Massillargues the hautboy player betook himself to his mother's potato patch one day, with his neighbor's old mule hitched to a plough. He sung out to the mule in the shrill tones of the hautboy, and the beast tore across the field like mad, dragging the boy and plough after him. He tried to quiet him down; but the more he heard of his notes, the faster he went — back and forth across the patch they had it, — and they might still be ploughing, if the plough had not struck a buried root, broken the harness, and sent the hautboy player turning somersaults into the middle of the potato patch. The poor fellow went home more dead than alive. His mother asked him how he came in such a plight — all sweat and dirt. He answered, surly as could be:

"'Never will I touch a plough again, — I have had ploughing enough to last a lifetime! N'aï fa un tibajé, un tibajé!'

"The story got out, and everybody calls him 'Tibajé.'

"The hautboy player of Fontade has a mean temper. He was always crying when a child, and his mother gave him sweets and bonbons to quiet him. The young rascal would stop long enough to eat; then he would cry louder than ever: 'N'en volé maï! N'en volé maï' (I want more). So it came to be his nickname. To be sure, he is rather surly when they call him 'N'en volé maï'; and, if he were not a hautboy player, he would get downright mad.

"But what can you expect? Hautboy players should be philosophers, and then — so long as the pot is kept boiling — that is the main thing. We work little, earn good wages, are always *en fête*. We dress well, and why

should we worry or get mad?   For my part, you may
often hear me singing:

" Tan pis pèr caou sé chagrina
Ieoù siéï toujoù gaï é countèn
É mé plasé din ma cousina
Surtou quan l'astié vira bèn." *

———

* Sorry for who grieves,
  I am always cheerful and content,
  And I delight in my kitchen
  When the spit nicely turns.

❖ ❖

Cypeyre of St. Clément
and Lou Douna
of Lecques.

❖ ❖

Cypeyre of St. Clément and Lou Douna of Lecques

WHILE Fougasse was relating his story, we arrived in the village, and he and the little drummer-boy took to our left. I wanted to spend the night at the inn, the wolf story had made such an impression on my mind. I took courage when my companion said: " It is true that in the days of which Fougasse speaks wolves were numerous, but in the last few years they have been hunted down. Now there are not so many, and perchance, if we come across one, we will whistle a tune, and find out whether there is any truth in his tale. Besides, this village inn is very poor. Let us push on to the next village. I know the innkeeper, and we shall be well treated." But I was thirsty, and insisted on having a drink, so he went to the inn with me. There was a solitary traveler in the room sitting before a bottle of claret. He greeted my companion with:

" Halloa, Cypeyre, is that you? What good wind brings you here? "

The other replied: " And how d'ye do? Douna, whence do you come? "

" I come from the fair of Picho Gallargues."

" Had you anything to sell? "

" No ; on the contrary, I wanted to buy my seed for the coming fall from the Gypsies. They alone had any for sale. But I have seen them play a trick which has cooled me. I tell you they are nothing but a band of thieves; the government ought to wipe them out, one and all, men, women, and brats.

"Do you know they have played a trick on poor Henri de Catalan which makes one think twice before having any dealings with them. The poor fellow, to raise some money, wanted to sell his white mule Falet— that big white mule, with ears going 'fliqua, flaqua,' seeming to beat time when he walks. You know, Henri is not over smart. He was walking, his coat over his shoulder, vest unbuttoned, the rope of the halter in his hand, and 'barisqua, barasqua'—without ever turning to see if his mule was following him, certain that so long as held the rope he had the mule.

"Not far from the market-place, he passed a troop of dirty Gypsies. Hardly had he got beyond the camp, when one of them stealthily crept to the mule, unbuckled the halter, put his head in it, and followed Henri, who, unsuspectingly, jogged along, leading a man in the place of his mule—and that clear into the mule-market.

"When they were in the midst of the crowd, the Gypsy pulled gently on the halter, and then more and more, until Henri turned round with a 'Get up, you lazy mule!' You can have no idea of his amazement

when he saw the shabby, dirty Gypsy, with his shock of a head in the halter.

"'What art thou doing here, dirty lout!'

" The Gypsy coolly and blandly replied:

"'My friend, for a crime I had committed, God changed me into a mule. It is a great misfortune for you that my time should expire this morning. If you had sold me yesterday, the loss would not be for you. But as the law forbids you to sell a man for a mule, farewell!'

" He left, and Henri stood there in a crowd of men, speechless, the rope in his hand, the halter on the ground, scratching his head, and wondering if he was dreaming. He was the laughing-stock of the whole fair. His mule was gone, and, crestfallen, he took his way back home."

When we had refreshed ourselves we left Lou Douna and set out on our way.

" I think I know who you are now," said I to my companion. " You are Cypeyre of St. Clément, the business manager of the castle—I have often heard your name mentioned; you have been long in your present position."

" Oh, yes," he replied; " the position has been held by father and son for more than eighty years, and I am on my way back from Montpelier, where I went to see the owners of the castle. They are growing old, and do not come often to visit their estate. When they want anything they send for me. They are always very considerate, and treat me as one of the family; but this time they paid so little attention to my wants that I had to remind them that I was hungry, in a way that covered them with confusion and which makes me ashamed of myself when I think of it. This morning, at about two o'clock, I took a cup of coffee and left home to walk to town. You know the distance is fully thirty-three kilometres, going by short cuts on pretty rough roads. I reached the master's house about half-past eight in the morning, dusty, hungry and well-nigh spent. I was announced, and when I was asked to go into the dining-room, where the old couple were, it was close to nine o'clock. As hungry as a bear, my stomach would go 'brrrou, brrrou' at times. They were seated at the table, with two large bowls of café-au-lait before them, some nice chicken and sausage, butter and rolls of fresh-baked pain-au-lait, which made one's hair curl, I assure you. I would willingly have eaten three or four, for I was hungry, and 'a good appetite requires no sauce,' they say; but I had to wait for an invitation which never came.

"They were both very kind. 'Oh, Cypeyre, you have not come for so long! Well, how is all at the castle?'

"'Yes, sir; all is well'—and I was invited to sit by the chimney before a bright fire.

"I thought to myself, 'I am more hungry than cold.'

"The gentleman said: 'The shepherd is now recovered, is he not?'

"'Yes, sir; he is well again.'

"'And the old mule lasts yet?'

"'Yes, sir; but we shall have soon to replace him.'

"'And the colt—he must be fine; he will soon be three years old.'

"'Yes, sir; he is a beauty. I have already driven him a few times; he will make a good roadster.'

"'And the wood-choppers—are they through?'

"'Yes, sir; they finished two weeks ago, and I bring you the money they left for you.'

"'That is well,' said he; and meanwhile this old couple were daintily picking at every dish, and poor me, more hungry than both together, watched them with my stomach going 'brrrou, brrrou.'

"After a moment of silence, the lady said:

"'How are the flocks doing—is there much increase?' And before I could answer her: 'Té! has the goat any kids?'

"'Beg your pardon, madame; I had forgotten to tell you—she has three kids, and three fine ones they are.'

"The lady turned to her husband and said: 'Do you hear what he says?—three kids! How do you suppose they suck? The goat has only two teats.'

"I gave the husband no time to reply, but hastened to say:

"'When two suck the mother, the third does as I am doing now—it looks on.'

"The lady, stung to the quick, apologized profusely:

"'Excuse us, Cypeyre; pardon us, my friend,—it did not occur to us that you had not had breakfast.'

"Promptly they gave orders to set a plate for me, and I was served like a king.

"I know I was somewhat rude, but you know:

> "'L'esprit quan lou vèntre baïssa
> Prén pa counsel qué dé la maïssa.'" *

I listened to all this without making any comment, finding Cypeyre's ruse bold indeed, and yet thinking that the oversight of the old couple deserved a little rebuke.

---

* An empty stomach guides the mind; or, an empty stomach consults only the palate.

❖   ❖

A Blind Man's Story,
or the
Miraculous Tree.

❖   ❖

A Blind Man's Story, or the Miraculous Tree

WHEN Cypeyre had done relating his story we walked in silence, until we reached the foothills of La Peña. There were two ways—the old and shorter road which goes over the mountain, and the new road which skirts it.

Cypeyre, who knew every inch of the ground in the country, said to me:

"Let us take the new road; a good road is never long to travel, and I wish to point out to you a spot where a very curious thing happened."

We journeyed on, and had skirted half the mountain, —we were then in the thick of the forest,—when Cypeyre pointed out a bare spot, and said:

"In olden times, on that clearing, was an enormous tree, which looked like a cedar. The lower branches, which grew on the trunk at a height of six or seven feet from the ground, were thick, straight, horizontal, and so long that a whole regiment could take shelter under them. Four men with outstretched arms could hardly have encompassed the trunk. The leaves were not needle-shaped, like the cedars', but were large and soft as velvet, and so thick was the foliage that one could look up and not see the sky through it.

"In summer shepherds led their flocks under this tree, to protect them from the noonday heat. At times five or six flocks could be seen under its shade, and there was room for them all.

"In winter few people traveled this region, the road was poor, the spot wild, lonesome, and dangerous on account of brigands.

"Every year in early springtime a great many "gavots" from the Lozère come down from their mountain homes to work in the rich surrounding departments, where they find more work and better wages than they could get at home.

"Two brothers, Batiste and Louiset, had gone to the Baumel farm, belonging to Monsieur Granier.

"Their work, which was paid by the day, consisted of spading vineyards.

"Batiste was seventeen years old, and his brother about fifteen. Besides their wages, they got wine and soup daily, cooked for them by the farmer's wife. The rest they furnished and prepared themselves; and the rest was little, indeed,— mostly codfish, bread, and cheese. But "gavots" are satisfied with little; and so long as the wine and bread last they do not worry. This coarse diet agrees with them, for when they come down in the spring they are thin, lank, and pale; but in a few days, although working hard, they grow fat and rosy.

"Batiste was headstrong. For him to stoop was seldom a pleasant task. His ribs must have run lengthwise, like a wolf's; at times you would have thought he had swallowed a sword, so hard was it for him to stoop and handle the spade. Louiset, on the contrary, was good, a hard worker, and, although younger by two years than his brother, he kept up with him in the work. He was, on that account, better liked than Batiste.

"In the country a well-known blind man went about begging, led by a small boy. Everybody gave him alms out of pity. He had his regular stopping-places in his circuit, of which Baumel farm was one. There he was always sure of a night's rest in the barn loft.

"Our two gavots were occupying it one summer night, when in came the blind beggar and his boy.

"'Say, Birèle,' broke out the blind man, 'let us count our money and see how much we have taken in to-day.'

"The boy began counting, and soon announced the result; eleven francs and ten centimes.

"'We are not rich,' said the old man.

"'But, grandfather,' said the boy, 'in the sack there must be at least fifteen sous' worth of bread.'

"'Oh! that is only eleven francs seventeen sous; it is small pay for our work,' replied the blind man.

"Batiste, who had been listening to their conversation, broke out:

"'You don't think eleven francs seventeen sous is enough for your work? Why, my brother and I work from early dawn until dark for five francs, and out of that we must feed ourselves; while you, I am sure, have not spent a sou for anything.'

" 'Yes, I bought two sous' worth of tobacco; no one is without his weakness, you know. But what we shall eat is a matter of no concern to us. We are given soup, ragoût, the remains of dinners, and all the wine we want. But I seldom take wine; it does not agree with me. They give us also money; some one, some two sous. The days are long; we beg at every door, and thus fill up our purse. Nevertheless, I am not satisfied with my day's work; it is one of the poorest.

" 'At the fair of Anduze, I have made as much as thirty-two francs; on the market of St. Hypolite, twenty-eight; at the Fête of Lezan, twenty-two. But the most I have ever made was at the Pilgrimage of Notre Dame de Prime Combe. I received, in sous, fifty-three francs eleven sous. You see, people under strong religious emotion are unthinking, and very generous. There is also much to be made at Notre Dame de St. Loup, at St. Gervasy, and other places. We don't miss a single religious fête. It is necessary, you see, to put something by for old age, and to *dot* one's children. Each one must fight his battles in the world as best he can, and, blind as I am, what could I do? My trade, after all, is worth another man's.'

" Batiste opened his eyes as big as saucers; he could

not sleep that night. The next day, when they were at dinner, he said to his brother:

"'Did you hear what the blind beggar said last night? His is a good business — twenty-three, twenty-eight, thirty-two, fifty-three francs in one day! Good gracious! And who knows if he tells the whole truth? If he lives a few more years he will have a fortune.

"'To put fifty francs aside it takes us at least a month, and the weather has to be fine every day for that — if it rains, we are behind hand; while he, rain or shine, takes in money.'

"Louiset, who was asleep during the talk between his brother and the beggar, was much surprised to hear this, and for a while was quite undone. After a moment's reflection, he said to his brother:

"'Certainly you are right; his business is better than ours. But he is blind, and we are not. To each one his lot on earth; and Father Grégoire told me for my first communion, that God had assigned to each one his work in the world, and we should never complain.'

"'Father Grégoire! Father Grégoire!' cried Batiste, 'if he was obliged to work as we do from morning till night, to live on codfish the year round, and never rest except on a rainy day — well, Father Grégoire would change his mind, I am sure, and speak differently. If you are willing, we can find means to live without working.'

"'How so? and what must we do for that?' said Louiset.

" 'If you like, I will put out your eyes; we will travel and beg, as the blind man does, and we shall have as much money as he has.'

" 'But you will hurt me.'

" 'Oh no; you will not feel it.' And so saying, Batiste took out of the fireplace a pine stick, and before Louiset had time to refuse his consent, thrust it into one of his eyes.

" 'Ouch! Ouch!' shrieked Louiset; and while he screamed "Ouch," his brother took another burning stick and thrust it into the other eye.

"The shrieks of the poor boy could be heard a mile off. He was wild with pain. He stamped and foamed in his agony, his face bleeding, his features convulsed. At this heartrending crisis, Batiste, in the coolest, calmest way, said to his brother:

" 'Come, now, don't make such a fuss for so little. I will apply a linseed poultice; it will relieve the pain; you will soon be healed.'

"Madame Granier, who had heard his groans, came in haste. When she saw him, she exclaimed:

" 'My poor boy, what has happened to you? Tell me.'

"Batiste hastened to answer for him: 'He climbed on yonder tree,' he said, 'to get a nest of starlings, and he fell on a brier-bush, and the thorns, I fear, have put out his eyes.'

"Madame Granier quickly sent for her physician, and while waiting for him, she applied sweet lard to

Louiset's eyes, and did all she could to relieve his suffering.

"The physician came, examined his patient, and said:

"'His eyes are damaged; they will still be pretty to look at, but the sight is destroyed. The thin skin of the pupil is gone; there is nothing to be done — the boy will be blind.'

"'Poor boy,' people said; 'such a fine fellow to be blind for life!'

"'It is awful! If such an accident had happened to his brother, we would not feel so sad; for he is such a mean fellow. But Louiset — poor Louis — good Louiset!'

"And, by way of comment, an old peasant added:

"'Anything would happen in this world, even to the death of a poor man's donkey, sooner than any mishap to such a tough as Batiste.'

"The physician treated the eyes the best he knew how, made the boy wear a bandage over them to keep out the light, in case the sight was not totally destroyed, and in three weeks the pain was gone; but the boy was entirely blind.

"All in the village took pity on him during his sickness. They provided for all his wants, and more, too. He, who had never been invited to sit at the table of any one in the village, was feasted like a king. He received attention and kindness, to which, as a human being, he was entitled before, but which no one thought of giving until his misfortune.

"The first emotion over, the villagers relapsed into their old somnolence, and Batiste and Louiset were at last obliged to carry out their plan.

"So, one morning they set out for a neighboring village, begging, for God's sake, from door to door.

"'Douna mé quicon, séouplè, quicon aou paouré avuglé, per l'amour d'aou boun Dïou,' plaintively entreated Louiset.

"'Gramerci, que lou boun Dïou vou lou reñde è vou bénigué,' added Louiset.*

"On seeing so young a lad in so sad a predicament, every housewife gave them alms. The first day they made fifteen francs thirteen sous, and in the evening Batiste said to Louiset:

"'You see what a sum we have. To earn that much we should have had to work three days. If this keeps up, we shall have a good business.'

"It kept up, and Batiste was full of care and kindness for his brother. He looked after all his wants, seeing that he lacked nothing. The best morsels given them were for Louiset. Every evening they counted their receipts, which kept increasing, and in a few weeks their purse was quite large. Week by week, and month by month, their fortune swelled, and by the end of the second year they had one hundred écus to their names.

---

* "Give me something, if you please, something for the poor blind man, for God's sake."

"Many thanks; may God return it to you and bless you." These are the words of entreaty and of thanks used by beggars in Southern France.

"But people born mean will sooner or later follow their inclinations. Batiste proved no exception; he got tired of this kind of life. 'To act as if one were poor, and yet be rich, that will not do,' he was always saying to himself; 'that cannot last. One hundred écus is a fortune. If I had not to drag that boy from door to door, I would go into some town, buy an old nag and cart, and peddle charcoal. I would soon get rich at that.'

"From the moment he began reasoning thus, he was not the same man. He began to steal from his brother half the alms, and when a choice bit was given them Batiste no longer shared it with his brother, but ate it all himself. Did some charitable soul give Louiset a good coat, Batiste put it on, and the blind boy went ragged. Louiset had worn-out shoes, while Batiste was always well shod. Kindness and tender care gave way to rough talk and harsh treatment, and many petty indignities, too sad to relate, were heaped upon Louiset by his brother.

"Louiset could not see it all, but he felt that he was not treated right; and one day something happened which occasioned a complete rupture. At the door of a nice house a large piece of omelet was given them — a delicious, golden-brown omelet, warm and fragrant — the odor would have revived a dead person. Batiste ate it all himself, and, taking Louiset by the hand, said: 'Come along.'

"Unfortunately for Batiste, Louiset had a good nose,

and the odor of the omelet made his mouth water. So he said: 'Give me a piece of that omelet; it smells good and must be delicious.'

"'Who told you I had any omelet?' gruffly retorted Batiste.

"'Who told me? I smelt it,' rejoined Louiset, angrily.

"Batiste denied having had any omelet; but Louiset felt sure that he had, and that he was deceiving him. Then he reproached his brother for causing his blindness, accused him of robbing him and getting rich at his expense, called him a good-for-nothing fellow, a rascal and a rogue, and was sure that God would punish his villainy.

"Batiste did not say much, but he was provoked, and promised to be even with him at the first chance.

"That evening, on leaving the village, they were walking along a foot-path which led through an old plantation of fine mulberry-trees, whose gnarled trunks showed their great age, when suddenly it occurred to Batiste that the spot was a favorable one to play a trick on his brother. He led him within two feet of one of the oldest and knottiest of the mulberry-trees, and told him to make a great leap to clear the ditch in front of him. The poor blind boy did as he was told, and jumping with all his might, knocked his nose against the tree, bruising his face frightfully.

"'Unnatural brother! Miserable villain! You wretch! where will your soul go to?' cried Louiset.

"Batiste replied, with cold brutality : ' You smelt the omelet; why did you not smell the tree?'

" From that time on, one thought possessed Batiste— to get rid of his brother. How to do it, was the question. To kill him would be a risk to himself, for murder will out; to abandon him might be worse, for surely Louiset would tell how his brother had put out his eyes; yet he had firmly resolved to cease dragging the boy after him.

" While in this quandary they reached, one evening, the very spot we stand on,— the country looked even wilder and more deserted than now. They stopped under the tree, and Batiste thought to himself:

"'Let me leave him here to-night; some wild animal prowling about will surely devour him, and no one will be there to tell the tale.'

"Batiste never slept over an evil thought—it would have been better for him if he had,— and at once set out to carry out his plan.

"'Sit under this tree, Louiset, and wait for me; I will soon be back,' he said. Louiset sat under the tree and patiently waited; his infirmity had taught him patience. He waited half an hour, an hour, and then began call- ing, ' Batiste! Batiste!' but Batiste made no reply. Growing impatient, Louiset called louder and louder, but the hills alone answered him. In the stillness that followed the echo of his voice, solitude was deep upon him. A chill crept over him as the thought flashed to his mind, and he realized that he was abandoned and

left to perish alone in a great forest. His soul became
a prey, in turn, to terror and anger, to utter dejection and
despair. His head in his hands, crouched under the big
tree, big tears left the sightless eyes of the poor beggar boy.
Night overtook him in that position, and a distant roar
warned him of danger near. The instinct of self-preserva-
tion gives courage to the most downcast of human hearts;
it filled Louiset with a sudden desire to live longer. He
sprang up, and tried to grasp the tree to climb it, but
failed; then, with the crook of his cane, he felt for a low
branch that he might pull within reach. He succeeded,
and, being nimble and agile, was soon perched on a high
bough in the thick of the tree. He was none too soon;
a wild boar grunted at the foot of the tree. 'Ah!' said
Louiset, with revived hope and a tinge of pleasure, 'what
a fine morsel I would have been for that fellow.'

"Just then the deafening tramp of thousands of animals was heard; they were coming from all directions,
and gathering under the tree.

"In the midst of that immense herd, with its confused
sounds, the roar of a lion could be distinctly heard.

"They greeted each other as they came,— animals
spoke in those days,— inquiring after each other's health
and about the ladies and the young ones left at
home. They paid compliments, and kept up a buzz of
conversation which reached Louiset's ears as articulate
sounds, but too indistinct to be intelligible.

"Louiset kept still on his branch, as though he was

petrified. His great fear was now to be discovered. To be discovered, indeed meant death, and a horrible death, at that.

"When all the denizens of the forest had gathered under the tree, and the tumultuous enthusiasm of the first hour had toned down, one of the crowd struck his paws for order and demanded silence. The confusion, as is customary in such cases, increased for a few seconds, as each one of the animals seated himself on his haunches; then all became still, and the lion, in a bass voice, said:

"'Friends, you know that we have not much time to give to our annual gathering; we have to retire before daybreak, and some of us have come from very far; so let us begin. What happened at Montpelier?'

"'Dame Zebelin, the widow of Mr. Zebelin, the fox, so well known by us, and so much dreaded by the chickens, was killed last week by her demented son. It is very sad, for she leaves three young orphans, who will fall a prey to the dogs of the neighborhood unless we try to protect them,' said a voice.

"'Let all the foxes of that district keep an eye on the little foxes,' roared the lion. 'Anything else?'

"'The youngest daughter of Mr. Catalan, the wolf, has eloped; her mother is heart-broken,' said a voice from the crowd.

"'When? when?'

"'No later than yesterday.'

"'With whom?—with a young wolf in the neighbor-hood?'

"'No, indeed; with an old fellow who has a large family of children, who is old and ugly, bob-tailed, and blind in one eye. His oldest son is after them, and, as he is in love with the girl himself, he will make it hot for the old man if he catches them.'

"'And he will serve him right—it is a disgrace to the animal family,' several said at once.

"'That is a good illustration of the proverb:

"'Fias prèstas a marida
Michan troupèl a garda,'"*

chimed in an old veteran, who was wearing a bandage over one eye.

"'What is the matter with your eye, Brother Groug-nare?' inquired the lion.

"'I have been driven from my lair so often of late by old Samalin's dogs that for a month I have slept with one eye open, and, no doubt, have strained my eyesight. On my word, I believe I'm growing blind!'

"'I know what will cure you,' said a falsetto voice, which Louiset thought must be a marten's.

"They all turned towards the last speaker, and an in-credulous smile wrinkled the scarred face of the old vet-eran of the woods.

"'What can you know, youngster, that I don't know?' contemptuously asked the old boar.

*Daughter of a marriageable age, bad flock to watch.—Proverb of Languedoc.

" 'I know,' piped the marten, while his tail was nervously switching the ground, ' I know that the leaves of this tree will cure sore eyes. Just rub them over your eyes for twenty minutes and see! Mother told me before she died that they had been known even to restore sight to the blind.'

" 'That's so,' said a sly old fellow in a tremulous voice; ' your mother and I were of an age, and I have known of the curative property of these leaves from my earliest youth; but I never mentioned it—it was a great secret—and you would have done better, youngster, to have held your tongue.'

" 'Perhaps so,' said the marten; ' but I only had in view to help a suffering brother—and, then, among ourselves, we ought to be able to speak out freely and fearlessly.'

" 'Aye, aye, I wish it so!' said the same tremulous voice. ' But remember, youngster, that prudence is the mother of safety; and you must be on your guard, for here stones have ears.'

" ' I know something,' said a wolf who was a traveling musician; ' but I should not like it to go beyond the present company.'

" 'Speak without fear,' said several voices; ' we will keep your secret.'

" ' Well, about a month ago I was in Corconne, playing the clarinet for a country dance. The day was hot, and my throat was parched; I was actually dying of thirst.

I asked one of the dancers for a glass of water. He laughed in my face, asked me where I was born, and whether I had cut my eye-teeth. "Don't you know," added he, "that in Corconne chickens die of the pip for the lack of water?"'

"'They brought me a glass of wine. I drank it, and it made me more thirsty yet. After the fiftieth dance, dry, hot, and out of wind, I strolled out, and chanced to stop under an old, half-dead cherry-tree, to cool off. Now, you all know that I inherited from my father the gift of finding water; that with my foot I can tell where a spring is, how deep in the earth it is, how much water it will yield, and all about it. Well, I was hardly under that old, half-rotten tree, when my foot struck it. The current was so strong that it made me dance a jig on the spot, tired as I was.

"'The dancers looked amused, and said I had gone crazy, but I held my peace. If they had not killed so many of my kind, I would have told them all about the spring; but now I want it kept a secret. Nevertheless, whoever finds the spring will confer a great boon to Corconne. Now, all of you keep mum about it, will you?'

"'We shall, we shall,' shouted they all.

"There was a moment's silence, then a voice, which might be the fox's, said: 'Friends, a year ago, in our annual gathering under this very tree, some of us criticised the medical profession as more baneful to mankind than we to chicken-coops; and yet I believe that physicians are improving in their methods, and are relieving suffering humanity. I wish we could take pattern after them, and study the art of curing our sick brethren, especially those who suffer from that dread disease — consumption. We are all liable to it, you know, on account of being out nights.'

"'Not all animals — not all by any means! Did you ever see a Billy Goat die of consumption?' grunted, with a wink, an old sinner of a bear, which saying raised a general laugh.

"'Yes,' retorted the fox, who was not slow at repartee, 'when you get him in your embrace, Master Bear, he does usually die of *consumption*.'

"The audience fairly roared. The bear gave a tremendous grunt, and looked his meanest at the fox, while the lion rapped for order.

"From the middle of the crowd arose an old patriarch, who, with calm dignity, said:

"'You have just heard from the lips of our cunning brother, the fox, that physicians had greatly improved, and could cure almost anything; but I tell you they do not, and there is a man who has very little faith in them.'

"'Who is that?' asked several voices at once.

"'Mr. Duran Palerme, Marquis de Castrie. Go and ask his opinion of physicians; he will tell you a different story.

"'His only daughter has been ill ever since she left

her convent.   She has been treated by all the physicians of Lyon, Marseilles, Montpelier, Toulouse, and Paris, but no one has found what is the matter with her.   They have treated her for all kinds of diseases; she has swallowed tons of drugs, and has cost her father a fortune. She is about nineteen years old, and would be pretty if she were not so thin; but she is fast losing strength, and cannot live long.

"' Her father has offered her in marriage to any young physician who will cure her; but so far no one has succeeded in curing her.'

"'I know what ails her,' said another; 'but it is a secret known only to myself and an old servant of the Marquis, whom he had dismissed just before the girl's illness. This old woman is in her dotage, and often thinks aloud.   One day, as I was hiding near her hut, I overheard her muttering to herself about the cause of the disease; and she chuckled with ghoulish glee at the near death of the young lady.'

"'Will she not relent in the presence of death?'

"'No; the old wench will not relent, even in the presence of death. You may depend on it, her heart is parched — lost to all humane feelings.'

"'Well, what ails the girl? Let us know it,' the meeting inquired, their curiosity at its height.

"' Not much, after all.   Under the left breast there is a lump as big as an almond, which drains her life-blood and exhausts her strength. If the lump were removed with some sharp instrument, she would be well within a month. No physician has ever seen it. It does not pain her, and she has not thought of mentioning it to any one. A maid-servant, who is something of a witch, discovered the lump while undressing her, and knew that some day she would have trouble with it.'

" 'That is strange, indeed. How many diseases the flesh is heir to!' philosophically remarked an old veteran marauder who sat near the lion. 'But it is now early dawn, and I would advise a speedy retreat into the thick of the forest.'

" They all arose, and the gathering broke up, with the understanding that they should meet next year on the same spot.

" For some time this great scattering of animals in all directions, in the stillness of early dawn, was something weird and awful. There was a rustling of dead leaves, a cracking of branches, and the general stampede seemed to give life to every bush within miles around. Little by little, however, the noise receded, growing fainter and fainter to the ears of Louiset, until only now and then was heard the cracking of branches in the distance; then all was still. Half an hour after the meeting broke up, Nature resumed her wonted stillness, and the most profound silence reigned over the primeval forest— silence the more impressive, that it succeeded the noisy tramp of ten thousand four-footed beasts, and preceded the awakening of sleeping Nature. The lull was soon

over. Louiset heard a lark, and a melodious note proclaimed to the winged denizens of the woods the dawn
of a new day. A thousand little throats answered,
the woods became astir with life, the sun kissed the dew
and dried every tear from the leaves, the flowers sent
up their fragrance—night was gone.

"Louiset was a country boy, and had seldom missed
a sunrise. He knew all the infallible signs of the dawn,
and, stretching his benumbed limbs, he began to breathe
more freely. He had not slept that night, I assure you;
but he had been a very attentive listener to the discus-
sions of the assemblage below.

"The revelation made by the marten filled his heart
with hope. Oh, if it only might be true that the
leaves of the tree which sheltered him could restore his
sight, how thankful he would be! His night of anxiety
on the high perch would prove a great blessing. He
lost no time, you may be sure, in feeling with the sensi-
tive fingers of a blind man for the finest and softest
leaves with which to rub his eyes.

"About fifteen minutes after he began rubbing, he saw
stars twinkling like diamonds through the leaves. That
gave him courage; he kept rubbing, and soon made out
the tree, then the woods, the road below, the beautiful
sun, which had been eclipsed for so long; finally the
least object about him became visible. With a joyous
shout and a thankful heart, he jumped to the ground,
found his bearings, and, with a song on his lips, set out
for the nearest village.

"On the way, he looked himself over, and found his clothes all rags and tatters, his shoes worn out, his hat brimless, and he the very picture of destitution. His brother had taken all the money but fifty francs, which he must have left by mistake. Fifty francs was not too much to refit him with good clothes; but he would not go to the best tailor — some second-hand clothes would do, for he must make the small sum go as far as possible.

" Late in the afternoon he reached a small town, where he inquired for a dealer in old clothes, and purchased a good-looking suit and a pair of shoes. He washed and brushed himself, then went to an inn for his dinner. He partook of an omelet as a reminder of his ill-luck, and treated himself to coffee and cigars in honor of his good fortune. Although Louiset was only a peasant, he had seen and observed good manners, and he sipped his coffee and lounged at his smoke as any gentleman would have done. There was no doubt about it, he was enjoying the new *rôle* immensely. Escaping from the jaws of death, as it were, he could not be more exultant over the turn in his luck. But Louiset was also a shrewd fellow. He remembered what Mr. Wolf and Mr. Fox had said about the great price the villagers of Corconne would pay for water, and the rich marriage in store for the young man who could cure Miss de Palerme, and he was laying plans to carry out successfully the two great undertakings.

" His coffee drunk, and his cigar smoked, he retired to his room and thought out again his schemes, and was in the act of marrying Miss de Palerme, when sleep overtook him. All that night happy dreams hovered over his pillow, and the sun was already high when he awoke.

"Remembering that diligence is the secret of success, he quickly dressed and breakfasted, paid his hotel bill with his last sou, and set out for Corconne, gaunt of wallet, but light of heart.

"This was on Sunday morning, and he reached the village in question as the last church-bell was ringing. A stream of people were pouring into the church, and Louiset thought:

"'I had better go in and attend the service, and after church I will speak to some of the people of my scheme to furnish the village with water.'

"Dipping his finger in the font, he crossed himself, and modestly sat on a bench near the door.

"In Corconne, a stranger does not turn up oftener than once in ten years; so his presence in the church made a sensation. A whisper went round, people turned to look, and the maidens stared at the stranger. Even the good priest noticed him, and, with native courtesy, shook him by the hand, and invited him to a better seat. Still more, he urged him to join the choir.

"'I am not a fine singer,' said Louiset; 'but I can sing a little.'

"The priest led him to the front row of the choir, and he did his best to sing; but they all sang out of tune, and

Louiset could only keep time to the chorister with his features. He did not know how they would like this kind of pantomime, and was frightened when he saw the priest coming to him after service. The latter did not notice his blushes, complimented his singing, and asked him to dine.

"Louiset thanked the priest, and accepted his invitation with pleasure, since he was penniless and eager to talk to some one of his mission.

"At table, after the bouillon, Father Poumier, who was a solid drinker, said: 'Let us drink a glass of claret,' and he poured the glasses full to the brim. Louiset thought his chance had come, and said:

"'Father Poumier, I am not much of a drinker; I would prefer a glass of water.'

"'Water!' exclaimed the priest; 'it is water you want! Rather ask for the jewels of the king's crown than water in Corconne! Water is what we lack most; and if any one could find a spring in the village, the mayor would pay him a handsome price.'

"'Do you really think they would pay the man well who should find a spring?' and Louiset scanned the priest's face.

"'Indeed they would!' was the earnest reply.

"'Well, Father Poumier, I must inform you that I came for no other purpose than to furnish water to the people of this village.'

"'Why, do you mean it? And how did you know we lacked water? Are you a wizard?'

"'Perhaps, sir.'

"'Well, I warn you that they will not fork over the money until they see the water gushing through the street. Large sums have been paid to hundreds of men who claimed to be water-witches, and we have dug up every foot of our public square, and many of the private yards, all without getting a drop of water.'

"'If I promise to find you a spring, I will find one; you may depend on it.'

"'Very well; after dinner we will step over to the mayor's — or rather let me send for him — ' and calling a servant: 'Please go ask the mayor to call here before going to the café; he will take coffee with us.'

"The mayor came, and they talked the matter over (that goes without saying); but the agreement they came to was this: The Commune would furnish four men and all the tools necessary to dig where Louiset should direct; and when the villagers had all the water they wanted to use, Louiset was to receive ten thousand francs, in three payments.

"The next day being Monday, the four men went forth with their spades and picks, followed by the villagers, to the public square. Everybody was dying to know where the stranger would break ground; and everybody was giving his or her opinion, as usual in such a crowd, when Louiset appeared, and going straight to the old cherry-tree, gave orders to dig it up.

"The ground around the old tree had never felt a spade, and the men had to use their picks. By nightfall they had only uncovered the first roots. The next day they removed all those which radiated from the stump, and they found the tree held by a single long tap-root. This proved that the tree had never been transplanted, but had grown on the same spot—a question which had long divided the village squabblers, and feeling ran high between the 'I told you so,' and the 'I never said it,' folks.

"At the root of the tree was a large, round stone. Two or three times this stone had blunted the axe of the workman. Louiset gave orders to remove it. The four men worked hard with crowbars. They pried it on all sides; they tried to lift it, and were about to give it up, when suddenly it was thrown up; a stream of water, three feet high and three feet in diameter, washed the four men out of the hole, and threatened to inundate the whole village!

"Everybody shouted: 'A miracle! A miracle!'

"The mayor, the priest, the municipal council, all agreed to raise at once the promised sum. A great feast was given in honor of the event, and Louiset was treated magnificently.

"The people of Corconne have since erected a monumental fountain on the spot where the old cherry-tree grew, and they have come to drink more water and less wine.

"Our Louiset, once in possession of the ten thousand francs, returned to town, and purchased a beautiful carriage and fine team, besides fitting himself with a handsome suit of clothes, silk hat and gloves, a physician's case, and a cane. Thus transformed, he seated himself in his equipage, powdered and spectacled, and ordered his coachman to drive him to the castle of Fourmagne.

"But oh, misfortune! A calamity had befallen the castle! All was commotion. The servants were coming and going, with sober faces and tearful eyes. Perceiving something unusual as he drove up, Louiset asked what had happened. He was told by the servants that their beloved young mistress had just died. He announced himself as a physician, and begged to see their master at once. Without delay, he was taken to the sick room. What he saw there moved him almost to tears.

" In a large, beautiful arm-chair, which had held the dying forms of many ancestors, lay the maiden, wrapped in an elegant *peignoir*, her head resting on a down pillow. She was, to all appearance, lifeless, and her father, the Marquis, was tearing his hair, wild with grief. Her mother, the Marchioness, was lying in a swoon, with maids trying to revive her.

"Louiset soon recovered from his emotion, and with a coolness that would have done credit to an old practitioner, he proceeded to take charge of the case. He felt her pulse, and found none; he placed his ear at her heart,

and perceived a slight beating. He asked for a hand-glass, and brought it close to her lips. It became veiled with a slight, a very slight cloud. Thus convinced that life was not extinct, he spoke in a commanding tone, at the same time with an assurance which brought hope to the Marquis' stricken heart:

"'She is not dead. Calm yourself, sir. And you, (to the servants,) don't stand there paralyzed. Place your mistress on yonder couch; give her plenty of fresh air, and open her gown at the chest.'

"The servants did as they were bidden, while he took out his case and applied a small vial to her nostrils, allowing her to breathe its contents; and lo! she opened her eyes and whispered faintly, as one in a dream, "'Ah! how well I feel!' and, to her mother who, revived, was now by her side, 'Be calm, dear mother; I feel so——' before the 'well' had left her lips, she had fainted again.

"'She is dead! She is dead!' they all cried.

"But Louiset commanded silence, and, addressing the Marquis, said:

"'Sir, your daughter needs perfect quietness. Let all retire but you and me—if we need more we will call,—and I will answer by my head for your daughter's recovery.'

"When they had all left the room, Louiset said to the Marquis:

"'Your daughter is very feeble; but she is not hopelessly ill. Trust her to my care for a month, and I

believe I can cure her. I do not profess to work mira-
cles; but I feel sure that I understand her case and can
give her exactly the right treatment.'

"'A dying man catches at a straw,' and the Marquis
was in that state that it took very little to revive his hope.

"'Sir physician,' said he, 'I intrust my daughter
to your good care. Do as you think best; and I repeat
to you what I have said to many other physicians: "If
you cure her, I will give her to you in marriage."'

" During this short colloquy, Louiset had applied the
scent-bottle again. When he had consent to treat her,
he unfastened the girl's dressing-gown, so as to expose
the left breast, and with a lancet, concealed in his hand,
he dexterously removed at a stroke the lump which,
according to the fox, was the cause of all the poor girl's
sufferings.

"This neat little operation performed, he waited a
moment. Presently she opened her eyes; and when she
had fully recovered from the fainting fit, he gave very
minute directions for the day's treatment. She was to
have good care, always by the same nurse. No one else
was to enter the room, and she was to take little besides
good beef-juice.

"'To-morrow,' said the would-be physician, 'I will
return and bring the sovereign remedy for her case; you
will see her stronger in a few days.'

" He took his leave of the Marquis, who remained
in a state of doubt and anxiety until the morrow.

"The following day, when Louiset came, he noticed that the patient looked better, and that her pulse was stronger; so he gave new directions to the nurse, and left a box of pepsin powder, which he called by such a complicated name that no one knew what it meant, not even the physician himself; but this powder, he impressed upon them, was the wonderful remedy which would cure infallibly, if given according to directions. So they did not bother about the name, but administered it to the patient as prescribed.

"The third day there was much improvement in the patient's condition. She relished her food, had gained a little strength, and even wanted to sit up. The Marquis and his wife were overjoyed; they treated Louiset like a prince, and reverenced him as the savior of their child. They insisted upon his staying at the castle, in order to be in constant attendance on their sick child, for fear of a relapse. Louiset refused discreetly at first, but finally yielded to their importunities, and became an inmate of the Marquis' household. It was not long before he was on the footing of a son at the castle.

"It would take too long to relate all the details of the damsel's convalescence, and to follow her through its many stages, as strength and beauty returned, and she became more and more an interesting subject of study for the young physician. Nor can I linger long over the sumptuous wedding at the castle after the damsel's full recovery. It suffices to say, that the blind beggar boy became the husband of an excellent and estimable lady; that he was henceforth on a footing of equality with the noblest and oldest families of the district; that his fame as a physician spread far and wide, and that, but for his common sense prompting him to take no more cases and to give up medicine as a profession, he might have had to answer at the Judgment Day for the death of many a person.

"As it was, he lived quietly and happily on his wife's income, spending much time in the Marquis' library, making up for deficient education, driving about with his wife, or riding with the gentlemen of the neigborhood.

"Some years later, he was, at the close of a hot summer day, inhaling the evening breeze from the broad piazza of the castle in company with his wife and their young child, the joy of his home, when a stranger, ragged and weather-beaten, stopped at the gate of the avenue and looked intently at him for some time, and then shouted at the top of his voice: 'Louiset! Louiset!'

"Louiset went to the gate, and was greatly surprised to see his brother Batiste; but as he did not care to present him to his wife, he took him to his private office and had a long conversation with him.

"To this day, no one has ever known what passed between the two brothers. The reproaches Louiset addressed to Batiste, the tears of repentance Batiste may have shed, the forgiveness he may have begged, are all for us to guess. All we learned from the interview

is the history of Batiste after he left Louiset under the tree.

"He took the road to Marseilles, and walked all night and all day, in order to get far away from his brother, and not to hear of his cruel death. But travel as far as he might, he seemed always to hear the agonized shrieks of his blind brother as he fell a prey to the animals of the forest.

"Reaching Marseilles, he carried out his long cherished plan. He bought a mule and cart, invested in charcoal, and behold him shouting through the streets: 'Charcoal! charcoal! who wants to buy any charcoal?'

"He made a good living. The sun shines on the just and the unjust, and he might have laid up a competency, had not his evil propensities led him into bad company. His friends, the vagabonds of Marseilles, robbed him, beat him, and left him for dead in the streets. A soldier's patrol took him to the hospital, and when he came out he had to beg his bread. He was not, however, dragging a blind man, and the alms which fell into his hat were few.

"Batiste was in extreme misery when he reached the castle of Fourmagne and found himself in the presence of his brother. He dared not question Louiset; yet he was very curious to know how his brother had come by so much wealth.

"Louiset told **his** brother very briefly all that had happened to him since they parted. He pictured his despair on finding himself alone in the woods in the night; his fear at the approach of the wild beasts; what he had learned from their conversation; and how, afterwards, he had made a fortune in marrying the daughter of the Marquis of Fourmagne. Overlooking past grievances, he gave Batiste a considerable sum of money and dismissed him.

"Madame Louiset, with feminine curiosity, wanted to know who that beggar was; but Louiset put her off with: 'Only one of the many workmen in need,' and the stranger was never seen or mentioned again.

"Batiste was hardly out of his brother's presence when he said to himself:

"'Why should I not go to the tree? The same animals will be sure to come, and they may tell other secrets which will be useful to me.'

"No sooner said than done. Batiste made his way to the tree; and on the evening of the first of May, we find him perched up on the branches, waiting for the animals to come.

"This time they did not exchange compliments when they met. On the contrary, there were many harsh words of reproach for the traitors who had let out their secrets. Such villainy had never been known before among the animal tribes. Some of their number must have betrayed the confidences of the last meeting, and, from words, they came to blows about it. The noise was frightful. The uproar shook the branches. Terrified,

Batiste tried to climb higher, when the rustle of leaves and swaying of a branch, betrayed him :

"Some one in the tree!" shouted a signal. "Some one in the tree! Some one in the tree!" was caught up by many voices.

At this cry the tumult ceased, and they all listened for another sound. Batiste was by this time chattering with fright, so that the branch creaked under him.

"Our betrayer is in the tree! Our betrayer is in the tree!" spread the angry cry.

Immediately an immense bear came out of the herd and climbed the tree and made for Batiste with all dispatch,— he was shaking like an aspen-leaf behind a big branch,— gave him a terrific blow with one paw, and sent him crashing down through the branches into the midst of the herd of furious animals, who made short work of him. And so, *pecaïre!* he was torn to pieces and devoured by the very beasts to which he had delivered his brother.

And the cock crew, and the story ended.

ALMOST always after a thrilling narrative, a dismal tale, or a fascinating story, there is a moment of silence. Whether the mind needs rest after the great strain, or whether it inclines to go over what it has heard, that I cannot say,—I leave the explanation to more learned men,—but the fact remains, that after hearing of the Blind Boy's thrilling adventures, Cypeyre and I walked a long way in silence, and hardly exchanged a word until we reached a spring under a willow-tree.

Some men were already sitting there in the shade, talking. One was from Manoblet, another from Cazagnole, a third from Gaïan, and others from Brogassarge. They welcomed us, and we soon fell into conversation. I asked the man from Gaïan, why the saying goes that *misery* is always at Gaïan?

He laughed, and said: " You must be from far, or you would not ask such a question; we have a family by the name of 'Misery,' very poor and very numerous; so it is not surprising that there is always plenty of misery at Gaïan."

Another spoke up, and said: "I wonder why all villages have their nicknames, and how they originated."

The man from Manoblet, replied: " Those appellations are, many of them, too old to know their origin; but I believe they came from some village custom, or some

peculiarity of the people. For instance, they call the
Lecquars, 'Brayers of Lecques;' because, at all times of
day, you may hear them shouting to the ferryman:
'Hey! halloa! come to ferry me across!'

"They call the villagers of Cannes, 'Shoers of cats,'
(ferra cats); and the story goes that, once upon a time,
the youngsters of Cannes caught all the cats, and stuck
nutshells on their feet with pitch, and turned them
loose in the streets. You can imagine the fun for the
cats and their owners.

"People of Lunel have long been known as 'Pesca
Luna,' (fishers of the moon). Tradition says that some
idiotic fellows were trying to fish the moon with a bucket
as it was reflected in the canal. As soon as the bucket
touched the water, the moon began to dance, and the
lookers-on said to the fisher: 'Go slow, or it will get
away!' And when the water was very still again, and
the moon in the bucket, they lifted it very slowly, and
tickled as schoolboys, started for the town with the moon
in the bucket. Unfortunately, they stopped to get
a drink at the tavern of Valatoure. A donkey passed
along, saw the bucket on the sidewalk, gulped down the
water, and, no doubt, with it the moon.

"They say 'Passeroun de Soumèire,' (sparrows of
Sommières), and this is why: Some men had loaded a cart
with long beams, placed crosswise. When they tried to
go through the narrow streets they got stuck, and did
not know what to do. The men stood scratching their

heads, when a sparrow flew past, holding in his bill a straw two feet long. The little sparrow was not as stupid as the three men. It held the straw by one end, and reaching its hole,— bisst! in it went.

"'Té!' said the brightest of the three; 'if it had held the straw by the middle, it would have got stuck as we did.'

"And quickly they laid the beams lengthwise on the cart, and passed through the street with no trouble."

Each one gave the name of the villages he knew, but there were so many I have forgotten most of them.

Finally, we all got up and started on our different ways at the same time. Cypeyre and I were bound for the same village, so we journeyed on together, and arrived at sunset. We secured the best two rooms of the inn, where Cypeyre was known, and while supper was being prepared, we strolled through the streets, and took a look at the place.

Women were out with brooms sweeping the streets with all their might. Men, with long ladders, were draping the sides of the houses, from eaves to pavement, with sheets, curtains, and tapestry. Girls were coming and going, running this way and that, bringing evergreen branches, sprays of bloom, and masses of flowers, seeming to have all the wealth of Nature in May-time at their disposal; while maidens and youths were arranging them in festoons and garlands fastened upon the draperies in graceful and artistic designs. The village

was evidently putting on holiday airs, and we were about to inquire what it all meant, when a cry arose:

"Help! Help!" And a few steps in front of us a woman rushed into the street with hair disheveled and face terrified.

The women, with their brooms, came to her rescue, with: "What is the matter? What has hurt you?"

But before she had time to speak, a man, with a broken stave in his hand, rushed after her, and proclaimed to them all, as if a great joke:

"My wife's a silly goose; she cries because I happen to break a stave!" and to the wife, consolingly, "Come now, don't make such a fuss over a broken stave; there are plenty more left." (He was a cooper.)

"That villain Petaras, he broke the stave on my back! he will surely kill me some day, the wretch!" cried she, while Petaras, all smiles, went into the house with the air of a hero.

The women all took her part, and crowded around her to hear the whole story. After this tragic scene we returned to the inn, thinking only of the cool brutality of Petaras.

❖ ❖

The Marriage of Monsieur Arcanvel; or, the Story of the Gloves of Louse-Skin.

❖ ❖

The Marriage of Monsieur Arcanvel; or, the Story of the Gloves of Louse-Skin.

AFTER supper, while talking of many things, I remarked to the innkeeper that I purposed to set out early the next morning.

"Why, you do not know, then, what is going to happen to-morrow!" exclaimed he. "We are forbidden to let any stranger leave town. The whole village will be in holiday attire. The expenses of the fête have already been paid. Villagers, strangers, one and all, are bidden to the wedding; for our squire marries his son to-morrow."

I sprang to my feet with surprise.

"But," he continued, "you do not seem to know anything about our squire. Well, he is the richest man in the country, and the kindest of the rich. He is not proud; he greets every one he meets, and never fails to inquire 'How d'ye do, and how's your family.' He daily visits the poor and sick, provides them with all they need, food, fuel, or medicine, and has always a kind word or good advice for the least of us. If any man needs a job, he has only to apply to the squire; he has work for every one on his estate, winter and summer; so we look up to him as our father. Never and nowhere is a better man to be found — nay, his equal is yet to be born! We would any of us go through fire and water for him; but all we can do is to repay him with kindness, and we all try to, except that rascal Petaras, who does not care a fig for the squire, and never listens to him. He is the only one who 'll not be present at the wedding."

I made bold to inquire whether the young man's bride was from a neighboring town.

"Oh!" said he, " it is quite a story. If you like, I 'll tell it to you. The evening is long; we shall have plenty of time for sleep after I am through; and I know you will not be sorry to hear the romance, for it will help you to appreciate what you are to see to-morrow."

"I have already told you that Mr. Arcanvel is very rich. He owns here the finest castle and estate for miles around. He has also many beautiful farms in the mountains, on which graze thousands of cattle. No one knows exactly how may people he employs, either on his home place, or in yonder Cevennes. Most of his income though is derived from his ships on the seas — and every year he takes a trip to Paris to receive his dividends.

"Two or three years ago, when about to set out for Paris, he was taken ill with rheumatism, which laid him up and prevented him from undertaking the journey. His son, a young man of about twenty, well educated, handsome, and as kind-hearted as his father, had to go in his place.

"One fine April morning, mounted on a superb horse, he set out on his trip. The first, second, and maybe the third day, all went well. In fine spirits and full of anticipation, our traveler journeyed northward, delighted with the prospect of seeing the capital; when about three o'clock one afternoon,—as often happens in spring,—the sky became very cloudy.

"At first he paid little attention to it; but he soon perceived that the sky was growing black with threatening clouds hanging on the hillsides, and a roaring was heard, which grew louder and louder. Soon a great wind arose, and blew so hard as to almost lift him off his horse. Night was approaching, the darkness increased, and the dust blinded him so that with difficulty he could make out his way.

"Suddenly there was a flash of lightning, then a second one, then a rapid succession of flashes, followed by a pelting rain, and by the loud and long peals of thunder in the neighboring hills.

"It was the beginning of a fearful storm, which kept increasing in fury, leveling trees, hurling rocks from the mountain side, and threatening to destroy both horse and rider.

"Poor boy! only to think of that fearful ride makes me shudder. I seem to see him yet — alone in the dead of night — with lightning rending the sky, and making the black night blacker yet, with the storm raging about him, and the rain beating down in torrents.

"The poor boy would surely have been lost, had not a kind Providence taken pity on him and made him discover, suddenly, by a flash of lightning, a large building not far from the road. It was the castle of Sérignac, the residence of Baron de Donan, a nobleman with one child — a daughter of eighteen. Arcanvel rang the bell of the lodge, and a servant, lantern in hand, came to see what was wanted. When the servant saw that horseman, drenched to the skin, he quickly opened the gate, gave him shelter, and hastened to inform his master.

"'My Lord,' said he, 'a young man, half-drowned, comes to ask for a night's shelter. What shall I do?'

"'Welcome him, of course, whoever he may be,' said the Baron; 'order the groom to take the horse to the stable, and see that he is well rubbed down, dried, and fed; and give the young man a warm room and dry clothing.'

"Young Arcanvel was delighted with all that was done for his comfort, and with the polite and respectful demeanor of the servants towards him, as they lighted a cheerful fire in his room, brought him dry clothing, and a glass of Chartreuse to revive him.

"'They must know who I am,' said he to himself, ' to treat me like this.'

"When somewhat rested, and quite dry and warm,

he was shown into the drawing-room, where the Baron awaited him, all impatience to know who the storm-stayed stranger might be.

"The Baron took the young man by the hand, and inquired whom he had the honor of addressing.

"'Mr. Arcanvel, of the castle of Vic,' said that gentleman, with an apology for giving his host so much trouble.

"'Oh!' replied the Baron, 'you do not inconvenience me in the least, you are very welcome, Sir.' Then turning to Lisette, the servant: 'Tell my daughter to come and have supper served at once, for Mr. Arcanvel needs refreshments, after his hard experience.'

"A moment later the young lady appeared, timid, but charming. They were introduced to each other, and, after exchanging a few polite words, they repaired to the dining-room.

"During the supper they talked a little of everything, as usual,—agriculture, industry, commerce, science, art, navigation, and lightly touched on politics. The young Arcanvel showed himself well informed on all subjects; he spoke, indeed, as if he had the mature experience of an older man. The Baron was pleased and surprised to find so much wisdom and knowledge in the stranger.

"Arcanvel told the object of his journey to Paris, mentioned his father's illness and his own suffering during the storm, 'to which I now owe,' said he gracefully, 'the pleasure of sitting at your lordship's table.' All this was so well said, in a pleasant voice and modest, refined manner, that the Baron could not help remarking to himself: 'That young man is smart, and he has had the right training.'

"Young Arcanvel was attentive and polite to Miss de Donan, as becomes a well-bred youth, and he made so good an impression on the father that it was very late when they bade each other a good-night.

"The next morning, when the servant called Mr. Arcanvel to breakfast, he found him in a burning fever. He had evidently taken cold. The Baron at once sent for his family physician, who pronounced it a case of pneumonia. Mr. Arcanvel's sickness was an event to be ever remembered at the castle. The physician did not leave his patient for a minute. He gave all the remedies known to science; he administered all the herbs of St. John, and applied all sorts of lotions; but, in spite of all that, for three or four days the young man's life hung by a thread. The Baron was in despair, — he gave up all hope. On the ninth day, however, there was a change, and on the tenth a slight improvement, and on the day following he was declared out of danger by the physician, and orders were given for the best care and perfect quiet, to prevent a relapse. The Baron had the orders carried out strictly, and insisted on overdoing, rather than to allow any neglect of the patient during convalescence.

"The young man's vitality carried him through, and

he improved rapidly. When he was able to take walks in the garden, the Baron permitted his daughter to cheer the invalid with her company, and the two were together a great deal, accompanied always by the maid, Lisette.

"Naturally, a friendship sprang up from this contact of two noble minds and pure hearts. The servants gossiped about them, of course; but Lisette, who was always present, declared there was no lovemaking.

"In spite of this, time and constant companionship were having their effect. The morning of the departure came, and the saddle-horse was brought to the door. The Baron wished a prosperous and happy journey, and the young man asked leave to kiss the daughter's hand as a token of gratitude. The Baron consented, if Miss de Donan was willing; and there was a graceful bow, a slight mutual pressure of fingers, as they were brought to the lips, and no one has ever known what passed through those fingers like an electric current, or what those two were thinking about as the horse's speed separated them; but, as for the Baron, he seemed to experience a great satisfaction on seeing his protegé start off rosy and well. His face seemed to say: 'You see, it is I who cured him.' And taking his daughter by the hand, they went into the park, climbed a stone bench, and waved their adieus as long as their cavalier was in sight, and he waved his hat until lost to view.

"After the departure of Arcanvel, all at the castle returned to their accustomed ways, excepting Miss de

Donan, who kept rising early, assisting Lisette in setting the table and in putting the parlor in order, as she did when she expected Arcanvel to breakfast.

" Her father noticed this, and thought to himself: 'My daughter is not the same girl since that boy set his foot in my house. Before his coming she was careless and childish; she had to be called an hour before breakfast, and was always late. Now she rises early, dresses quickly, sets her hand to everything, and is as alert as a gazelle. That's what it is to keep company with people of good manners and education. In the company of that young man she has improved a hundred per cent.; she has become elegant, like her dear mother — she has her voice and feature, but not her disposition.

"'My wife was a good woman, but obstinate, and when she was set on a thing, she was *set*, and there was no budging her.

"'My daughter has my disposition; she is all meekness and submission.'

"Poor Baron! Little did he suspect that his agreeable guest had sown in the heart of his daughter a seed which would become a great tree, and which all his paternal influence could not succeed in uprooting.

" The Baron was a widower, I have already said. The Baroness had died when their child was young, so a nurse had to be found. It happened that Lisette, a poor woman of good family, had just lost her husband

and an only child, and the Baron sent for her and gave
her entire charge of the little girl; she is with them
yet, as Miss de Donan's maid.

"One day, when the child was about three years old,
the nurse was combing her hair, and found two lice.
She placed them on a white cloth, and gave the child
a lesson in cleanliness; but she was delighted, took them
to her father, and asked if she might tame them.

"'What an idea!' said the father; but, as he never
refused her anything, he let her keep them. They were
placed in a box and fed on raw meat. They grew to an
enormous size, and had a beautiful skin of soft, reddish-
gray, like a mole's, sleek and shiny as satin. She kept
them for many years. And one summer, when she
came home from boarding-school, she asked her father
to have gloves made out of their skins.

"'That is one of your queer notions,' said her father;
but, as usual, yielded to her wish. The poor lice were
brought out of their pen and killed, their pelts tanned
and made into gloves. She wore those gloves on all
great occasions; they were much admired, and no one,
except the Baron and Lisette, could tell of what they
were made.

"About three or four weeks after Mr. Arcanvel left the
castle, he wrote a letter to the Baron, telling him of his
successful trip to Paris, of his near departure for home,
and thanked him once more for his great kindness, and
expressed his everlasting gratitude.

"The Baron was more than pleased,— men are always glad to be thanked for favors they have done,— and he sent word at once for young Arcanvel to stop on his way home, which invitation the young man expected, and eagerly accepted.

"Miss de Donan watched for him early on the morning he was to arrive, and when, from her window, she saw him turn the bend of the road on the top of the hill, she hastened to tell her father, who went to the porter's lodge to meet him, and received him as a father would receive his own son. When Arcanvel met Miss de Donan, it was not without emotion; but, like a polite and refined gentleman, his self-control kept back what his heart would have prompted him to say.

"Arcanvel staid but three days at the castle, for his father was anxiously waiting to see him, and to hear all about his son's trip and the settlement of his affairs. Three days were enough, however, for the young people to have an understanding with each other.

"In her youth, the late Baroness had a dear friend, who married the Marquis de Pieredon five years before she married the Baron. The Marchioness had a son and the Baroness a daughter, and they used to exchange compliments about their babies. One day, for fun, the Marchioness suggested that the two should be betrothed. What was said in joke was taken seriously by the Baron and his wife, and they all agreed to remember their promise at the proper time.

"What was more natural than to entertain thoughts of such a prospect! They were dear friends, both of noble family, their fortune about equal, their estates adjoining. It was a dream of happiness long cherished, which the death of the Baroness did not dispel.

"When the Marquis came to remind the Baron of his old promise, the girl being of marriageable age, and the Baron laid the matter before his daughter as his and her mother's plan for her, Miss de Donan fairly sprang to her feet. The Marquis was old; he was too short; he was no talker; he was as dark as a mulatto and awkward as a duck; was mannerless, and what not. 'I don't want him! I don't want him; I would rather die in the skin of an old maid than to marry him!'

"The poor Baron was dumfounded. He had counted on his daughter's sweetness of temper, on her obedience; he had always thought her disposition yielding, like his, rather than stubborn, like his wife's; he could hardly believe his eyes — that bound of his daughter's surpassed any of his wife's outbreaks. He was disconcerted, but still trusted that time and reason would change her mind. Alas! the poor Baron would find out when her mind was set, it was set, and that she was her mother over again!

"One day he ventured to reason with her: 'What are you thinking of to refuse a suitor like the Marquis? His parents are our neighbors and our friends,— they have a great name, are richer than we. What more do you ask? If he is a few years older than you, what does it matter? A husband had better be older than younger than the wife. Now, if you have any good reason for refusing him, let me know it.'

"'Well, father,' said she, 'I do not want to displease you; I am very sorry to go contrary to your wishes; but I love Mr. Arcanvel, and I shall not marry if I cannot marry him.'

"You can have no idea of the Baron's wrath on hearing this, nor of his vociferations against Arcanvel. He was a blackguard, a traitor, a seducer! That, under a feigned politeness, a seeming gratitude, which he was pleased to call eternal, he should conceal such base villainy, one could not conceive! Such a misalliance would be the everlasting disgrace of the family! Arcanvel! Arcanvel! What is he? A nice man, indeed! If, perchance, he was a scion of the humblest nobleman — well, perhaps, it might do — but, Arcanvel! — a plebian! No; never would he consent to such a marriage!

"From that time on, there was a great coolness between father and daughter. At table during mealtime they exchanged not a word. The Baron still hoped, and the daughter became firmer in her determination every day. With the cunning of a girl in love, she found means of corresponding with her lover. Her trusty Lisette proved her ally and accomplice. Honest soul as she was, woman-like, she enjoyed mixing in another's love affair; so every morning she met the postman at the gate of the park, gave him her mistress' letter to mail, and brought back Arcanvel's. Father and daughter lived thus for some time, each one waiting for the other to broach again the burning subject which divided them.

"One day, the Marquis of Pieredon came to renew his demand for his son, intimating this time that, if a prompt and favorable response was not given, his son would marry another.

"The Baron found himself compelled to break the silence first. He took her aside, and, with all the self-restraint that a man provoked by an obstinate daughter can command, he pressed the suit again. She would be rich and influential, and her sons would be powerful in the government, and all that. He spake long and earnestly, using all the tact of a diplomat to obtain her consent.

"The daughter listened with perfect composure, and when her father had finished, she said, in her natural, calm tone: 'Father, for the second time I must tell you that the Marquis does not please me. I am sorry indeed to have to go contrary to your wishes; but I would rather stay single all my life than consent to have the Marquis for a husband.'

"'Stay single all your life!' exploded the Baron, with anger rising in his throat, and a voice loud enough to raise the roof. 'Stay single all your life! But I insist on your marrying. You think you can drive me to let you marry that ungrateful knave Arcanvel. But you shall not have him.' And, with louder tone and threatening gesture, he added: 'You shall marry the first man who guesses of what skin your gloves are made, even if that man be a lousy tramp!'

"The Baron thought to frighten his daughter into submission; but when the sonorous echoes of his voice had died away, she calmly looked up in his face, and said: 'I accept, on one condition — the Marquis shall not be a competitor.'

" To this the Baron agreed, and soon through all the country it was known that on the first of May — the birthday of Miss de Donan,— at ten o'clock in the morning, all the suitors for her hand should rendezvous at the castle for the great guessing contest.

" All sorts of men — men from every station in life — young men, old men, rich men, poor men, noble, peasant, and beggar were invited to try their luck.

"The Baron hoped by the first of May to see his daughter change her mind and marry the Marquis, rather than take her chances of wedding the first-comer. In this he was also deceived. Miss de Donan awaited the day with a lover's impatience, confident that Mr. Arcanvel would come and win her.

" Early in the morning, on May first, they began to arrive, by twos and by fours — men from the country around. The well-to-do rode in buggies and dog-carts; the rich were driven in fine equipages by liveried servants; the farmers rode their work-horses; some peasants even came on donkeys. But by far the greater number came on foot.

"By ten o'clock, this motley crowd of bachelors, widowers, or whatever — some with a foot scarcely out of the cradle, and others already with one foot in the grave — had filled the court to overflowing.

"The most conspicuous figure of them all was a mendicant, with a dirty wide-brimmed hat on his head, long, greasy locks which fell to his shoulders and half-hid his face. He wore a gray linen shirt, which reached to his ears, and a cheap serge coat. He carried a pack on his back, and a gourd-shell hung at his left side; in his right hand was an immense cudgel, and on his feet were hobnailed wooden shoes, so heavy and clumsy that, when he walked on the paved court, one would have said it was the tread of a gendarme's horse.

"The whole crowd stared at him, but all avoided contact for fear of the vermin which might find refuge under his hat.

"From early dawn, Lisette had been on the watch for Mr. Arcanvel. She was greatly disappointed not to see him in the courtyard.

"Precisely as the last stroke of ten from the ancestral clock in the hall died away, the Baron stepped to the landing of the courtyard stairs and said curtly: 'Gentlemen, the time for the contest has arrived. Please enter.'

"The servants in charge of the suitors took them

one by one to Miss de Donan's boudoir, where she awaited them with the precious gloves on. As each one came in, he bowed to the young lady, looked at the gloves, gave his guess, and went out.

"By twelve o'clock they had all tried but one; yet none had given the right guess. This pleased the Baron, who would have been very sorry to see his daughter led away by any of them. It pleased also the daughter, who still hoped that at the very last minute Arcanvel would appear.

"The big dirty beggar, who until now had made no attempt, reached the door to enter. The servants barred the way, and bade him begone.

"The Baron was appealed to. Being a man of his word, he said : 'I wish no discrimination. This contest is open to all. So take him to my daughter.'

"Perforce, the servants had to obey, and the beggar went in, halting and hobbling. His ironclad sabots slid on the wax floor, and he plunged in all directions, while the servants were splitting their sides with laughter, and the fine furniture was in danger. Finally, he reached the boudoir, and said in a stentorian voice : 'Show me your gloves, please, Miss.'

"More dead than alive for fear that this one would guess right, the poor miss lifted her hand for the beggar as she had done for the others.

"'Well,' said he, 'your gloves are made of louse-skin. I have seen so many in my hat.'

"When it was known that the beggar had guessed right, all those who had not yet departed were for kicking the fellow out of the yard; and they advised the Baron not to give his daughter to such a dirty lout.

"The Baron had a high sense of honor, and he replied to them: 'I cannot break my word with this man. I give my consent to her going with him. It now rests with her to say what she will do.'

"Miss de Donan, fearing the Marquis more than the beggar, said: 'My word is also given. I submit to my fate.'

"Asking her future husband's permission to prepare for her departure, she retired to her room, hastily got a few things together, and came out ready to go. In a firm voice, with dry eyes, and a face set with strong resolution, she met her father coldly, bade him good-by, and left.

"Lisette hung to her neck and tried to detain her, but gently disengaging herself, she started off with her beggar. They crossed the courtyard where as a child she had so often played; they traversed the garden in which her favorite flowers bloomed; they hastened through the park under the shade of stately trees where she had dreamed her maiden dreams and pledged her love to Arcanvel. At the great iron gate she shook hands with the porter, and, without even turning round, passed out into the dusty road, to follow the destinies of a man she knew not, and to follow him whithersoever he would choose to lead her.

"Put yourself in the place of the poor maiden, and, if you have any heart, you will understand what she must have felt. For Arcanvel she had given up the most brilliant marriage and all that goes with it — comfort, ease, luxury,— and he had basely chosen to stay away from the *guessing contest*, and abandon her to the tender mercies of a dirty beggar.

"To describe her feelings, or depict her anguish, would require a talent far superior to mine, and a far deeper experience of life than I possess.

"The beggar and the bride walked for some time in silence, side by side. Presently, he asked her if walking tired her too much. She curtly replied, 'No, thanks.' They kept on their march until about sundown, when they came to a thrashing-floor with several stacks of straw. They sat at the foot of one for some time; then the beggar said: 'Wait for me here while I go to yonder farmhouse to get something to eat.'

"He went, and soon returned, carrying a small basket in one hand. To her surprise, he took out of it a clean napkin, two mutton-chops, still smoking hot, a bottle of wine, and two crystal goblets.

"'Eat,' said he, 'you must be hungry.'

"The conditions of her leaving home, and the emotion she had gone through had taken away her appetite; but to oblige her courtly beggar, she ate part of a cutlet, drank a sip of wine, and waited patiently until her companion had finished. He took back the basket to the farmhouse, and returned to make preparations for the night.

"Where and how the night was to be spent, was a question which filled her heart with terror. The beggar said nothing, but with his two hands went to work and dug a hole in the straw-stack, deep and wide enough for one person to lie comfortably in. Then he pulled out of his pack a woolen blanket and a clean, white, sheet. These he carefully spread out on the straw inside the hole.

"'You may go in and lie down and rest, while I sleep outside,' he said.

"She, who was accustomed to all the comforts of a bed of luxury, and to all the little attentions of a faithful maid, crawled into the hole in the stack at the bidding of a tramp!

"She had a few broken naps on that never-to-be-forgotten night. At the break of dawn, the beggar, who was guarding near the entrance to the hole, stepped away, and only returned when Miss de Donan came out with her toilet made. Taking out of his bag a modest, but clean breakfast, he offered it to his companion, who took a little food, and set out with him on their journey.

"They walked without talking much; but the beggar was very considerate and attentive to her little wants. A few days were thus spent journeying. Resolved to ask no questions, and to bear her fate without a murmur, she blindly followed him in a ceaseless march.

"One afternoon, as they were crossing a magnificent wood, they came upon some very large flocks of sheep, ewes and lambs. Under a large tree, sitting on the soft grass, one of the shepherds was playing his fife. He drew from his rude instrument the most melodious sounds. The distant woods echoed the simple melody, and Miss de Donan stopped to listen, delighted. The beggar, unnoticed by her, was watching her every motion, while he stepped to the tree and spoke to the shepherd: 'You fellows must have little trouble with your flocks, or you would not be piping away so merrily.'

"'Yes,' said the boy; 'my leaders are well trained. I would have little to do, and should be perfectly happy, if it were not for that mean black sheep yonder. She is as cunning as a fox, and gives me no end of trouble. So long as my eye is on her, she stays with the flock; but let me turn my back, and off she is poaching on the neighboring wheat-fields. I have been at my master to sell her; but he won't hear to a word of it, for she was his child's pet lamb.'

"'What is your master's name,' inquired the beggar.

"'Don't you know who my master is? Mr. Arcanvel! All these woods belong to him. All the flocks you have seen are his. He is the richest man in the country.'

"At the name of Arcanvel, Miss de Donan's eyes filled with tears.

"The beggar noticed it, and hastened to say: 'Do not worry; you will be very comfortable at the house. Let us proceed on our way.'

"On that same day, they came across large wheat-fields, so great in extent that the eye could not compass them.

"'Do you see those wheat-fields?' said he to her. 'They are Mr. Arcanvel's!'

"Another tear moistened her eye, and he again hastened to say: 'Don't worry; you will be very comfortable at the house. Let us proceed on our way.'

"Farther on, they passed by an immense vineyard, with fully a hundred men at work in it. Some of the men seemed in a very happy mood, for they were singing or whistling; others had fallen out with their teams, and were swearing at them; and still others were merely intent on their work, cleaning the ploughshares at the end of the furrows.

"This animated scene seemed greatly to interest Miss de Donan.

"The beggar noticed it, and broke out again with: 'Do you see this vineyard? Well, it is the property of Mr. Arcanvel.'

"A blush crimsoned her cheek.

"'Don't worry,' for the third time, said the beggar; 'you will be very comfortable at the house. Let us proceed on our way.'

"They walked a while, and found themselves in the midst of an immense luxuriant meadow, and they saw many men with scythes mowing the grass, and other men carting away the dry and fragrant hay. Women and girls were raking after the carts and bantering with

each other, singing gayly to the breeze of that perfect
May-day, and sending forth to the hills their peals of
merry laughter.

"This time, Miss de Donan was first to speak; and,
addressing the beggar, she said: 'Doubtless, all these
meadows must belong to Mr. Arcanvel.'

"'Yes, yes,—and many more besides. But don't
worry; you will be very comfortable at the house,'
responded her companion.

"A moment later a magnificent castle was seen
through the trees.

"Said the beggar: 'Yonder, behind the trees, is Mr.
Arcanvel's castle.'

"'Don't let us go there,' piteously entreated Miss de
Donan.

"She did not want to meet the man she fondly loved,
just at this juncture, when her emotion was so great,
and the beggar at her side so dirty.

"'Why not?' replied the mendicant quietly. 'He is
a very charitable man; he will certainly give us something to eat. Let us go.'

"In her confusion, she found no ready excuse, and so,
willy-nilly, on she was led towards the castle.

"From the gate started many avenues and alleys
diverging in different directions through the park. The
main one leading to the castle was lined with majestic
sycamores, hoary with age. On each side of this avenue
were diverging alleys of pine-trees, and the breeze playing

through them, gave soft, restful sounds. About the pine-trees were a great variety of shrubs.

"They had hardly got within the park gate, when the beggar turned toward Miss de Donan and said, pointing to a bush in one of the pine alleys: 'Té! rest under yonder bush and wait for me. I will be back soon.'

"She did as she was told, and waited. In about half an hour she heard the rumbling of carriage-wheels on the smooth gravel road. At the thought that it might be Mr. Arcanvel her poor heart began to beat almost to breaking. She hid as well as she could, that she might see and not be seen.

"The carriage reached the gate, but, instead of passing through, a handsomely dressed young man pulled his fine iron-gray team into the pine alley, drew up rein in front of her bush, and quickly alighted. It was Mr. Arcanvel himself! She recognized him, and, overcome with emotion, fainted. He caught her in his arms, bore her gently to the carriage, and drove at once to the castle.

"Miss de Donan came to herself in a sumptuously furnished room. Maids were attending, with smelling-salts and cordials, and bathing her head with a restorative.

"Beside her soft couch knelt Mr. Arcanvel. She gazed on her surroundings as in a sweet dream; then an expression of pain crossed her features, and she faintly asked for the beggar.

"Of beggar there was none, other than Mr. Arcanvel, who, to avoid detection, had dressed himself in the garments of one of his shepherds, donned a wig and beard, and made himself as grimy and unkempt as possible.

"When the truth dawned upon her bewildered senses, she drew him gently to her, clasped her white hands about his sinewy neck, and whispered with charming emotion: 'Oh, my love, my love, how much anguish my poor heart has suffered! Oh, cruelest and dearest of lovers, what have I not endured for thy sake!'

"'Be calm, my love. Later I will explain it all to you,' said Arcanvel, passionately.

"The following day, Monsieur Arcanvel Senior set out early for the Baron's. He went with many misgivings, but found a meeker gentleman than he expected. The Baron had been harsh and unyielding as long as his daughter was with him; but, as soon as she had left with the beggar, remorse entered his heart. He was not willing to call her back, but he sent out spies who brought him a daily report of their wanderings; and when he heard that she was at the castle of the Arcanvels, a great weight fell from his shoulders.

"Hardly was Monsieur Arcanvel introduced, when the Baron exclaimed: 'I know what brings you here. You have been shrewder than I. Your son has played me a smart trick. Well, I forgive him — and her as well. Now, sir, when shall we celebrate the wedding?'

"'When it may please you, sir,' replied the former. 'Would the twenty-fifth of May be too early?' And the twenty-fifth — that is, to-morrow — was agreed upon."

"But why did not Mr. Arcanvel make himself known sooner to Miss de Donan?" I asked.

"Why? Well, you are like many people who blame him and charge him with needless cruelty. They say that after the *Guessing Contest*, he ought to have made himself known, or at least as soon as they had left the castle. Now, Mr. Arcanvel is a man of tact and good sense. To act as he did he must have had good reason.

"It is my notion that to have made himself known right after the guessing match would have got him into trouble. The Baron would have suspected a plot, flown into a rage with his daughter, and most likely prevented her from leaving the castle. If Arcanvel had announced himself after leaving the castle with the girl, it might have lessened the distance that he meant to keep between them until he could claim her before the world as his bride. Arcanvel has never explained it to any one but Miss de Donan, and she has forgiven him. If anybody wants to find fault with him, let him do better if he can, I say.

"As soon as the wedding-day was settled, invitations were sent out to all the villagers, all the strangers, and the whole aristocracy of the country. You will see to-morrow the Comte de Barbusse, the Marquis de Gariguebasse, the Baron de Fonsemale, the Chevalier de Pio Grand, the Sire de St. Géli, and many others.

"The castle is being repaired from cellar to garret. There are perhaps one thousand workmen at it. I have not seen the preparations; but everybody agrees in saying that to-morrow will be a day never to be forgotten. They say that all the fountains have been stopped, and the reservoirs cleared of moss and swept perfectly clean, because the Baron wants the basins so clear that the young couple shall see their reflections in them."

The innkeeper ceased talking, looked at the clock and said:

"It is late. You must be tired. You had better go to bed and sleep soundly until to-morrow."

He arose, shook me by the hand, gave me a Roman lamp, and I went to my room.

I was not long in going to sleep; my day's tramp had fatigued me. And I had taken only one stitch, when the boum! boum! of the firing of anvils awoke me. The sun was already high. I hastened to dress, and went down stairs. The game-keeper of the castle was about the street inviting the new-comers to the wedding. He had found two merchants of Toulouse linen, one merchant of St. Quintin's porcelain, one onion-vender, a knife-grinder, and Matthioù, a ragman. We all set out for the castle.

By ten o'clock everything was ready; the guests were

all at the castle, and the gay procession began to form. They were to march through the village to the church, where the ceremony was to be performed, and back again to the castle. A master of ceremonies arranged everything to perfection. Four maidens arrayed in white, carrying huge bouquets, led the way; then came Baron de Donan and his daughter, young Arcanvel and his mother, M. Arcanvel and a sister of the Baron, the provost, the relations and guests in order of rank, then myself and a cousin of the provost, the villagers with their wives, and finally a lame and a blind man wound up the rear of the long and gorgeous procession.

Children in holiday attire lined the streets of the village, clapping their hands as we passed and shouting, " Long live the bride and groom! " The gentlemen pelted the children with dragées and bon-bons,— a lively scramble began. Like a flock of birds, they fell on the dragées, all in a heap, were up in a flash, and were rushing pell-mell after another handful scattered in another direction.

At church not a third of the invited guests could find room; the rest found diversion outside. The Sire de St. Géli, an elderly bachelor, who was fond of girls and jokes, held up a pretty cornucopia filled with choice candy, and adorned with ribbons, and announced that it was the prize for the girl who would be bold enough to kiss him.

Laughter and cheers greeted the Sire's proposal, but

became an uproar when a dozen maidens fell on the bachelor's neck, to his great confusion and embarrassment.

When the bridesmaids emerged from the church they were followed by the newly married pair; the procession reformed and began the return march. The village wives had slipped from the ranks, and all through the narrow village streets we were showered with rose leaves, violets, and bouquets of fragrant flowers, which fell on our heads from the upper windows, and covered the ground at our feet.

When we reached the castle, the bridal pair passed into the grand reception-room, and there, under a canopy of flowers, received congratulations from everybody, great and small, high and low; and then all went to partake of the wedding feast.

M. Arcanvel, who never did anything by half, had an immense tent erected on the lawn to supplement the dining-room. It was made of a silken fabric, adorned with drapery and paintings, and the tables, spread with the richest of linen and china, fairly groaned with the weight of the feast. To tell you about all the dishes served and the wines drunk would take too long; besides, I cannot remember half the names on the *menu;* but we were four hours at table, and at the end of the repast we suddenly discovered that the fountains in the park were playing jets of wine. A murmur of wonder and admiration spread through all the company as they witnessed the sight. The slender columns of red nectar reaching the leaves of the trees and falling back in droplets and spray, seen through the oblique rays of the afternoon sun, was the most fairy-like thing I have ever seen.

A troop of musicians, ensconced in a clump of trees, discoursed sweet music, and the rising and falling murmurs of the waters flowing over the rocky river-bed added their charms to the scene.

Dancing followed the feast, and illuminations followed the fading day. Through the open house and grounds we strolled in pairs and groups, viewing the beautiful sights and joining in the merrymaking until a late hour, when, amidst shouts of blessing and praise to the newly married pair and to the good squire, so much beloved by his people, the crowd dispersed.

Such a wedding was the talk of the country for months afterwards, and it became proverbial for its splendor and for the great number of guests.

All of us went away greatly delighted, agreeing that it was the event of our lives. The blind man said that in all his life he had not seen such a day. Matthioù, the rag-peddler, was a little gay,— no wonder! the water had been changed to wine,— went about the village street shouting his " rags, sacks, and bottles " at an unseasonable hour of the morning. Going to bed very late, of course, I slept most of the following morning, breakfasted as usual, and sauntered out for a walk.

There were no portentous omens, and I hope to die if I had the least idea of what was about to happen.

Strolling about the streets, I happened to see at a window the young lady who was my partner at the wedding, and on the doorstep, my friend the provost. I was invited in, and the young lady and I were left to ourselves. We talked over the wedding and of many other things. How it all happened, I don't exactly know, but before we knew it we had planned our own wedding for the near future. I dined with her and her friends and returned to my inn late in the afternoon.

The innkeeper, who missed me at dinner, had made inquiries and found out that I was at the provost's.

"That young fellow is going to make the fatal plunge," he said to his guests. When I appeared, he pretended to be surprised; he circled around me, raised my arms, opened my vest, examined me carefully, to see if there were anything amiss. I saw the twinkle in his eye and let him go on. Then, with mock seriousness, he said:

"Come now, this is not fatal! I see no blood; the arrow only went skin deep. If it had reached the heart you had been lost."

"Oh," I laughed, "people don't die of that,—not immediately at least."

"No," said he, prophetically; "but men are like moths that circle round the flame; they draw closer and closer, until they burn their wings."

The day after my betrothal, I started on my way home. It was sunrise in the month of May. The plain along the river bank was dripping wet. On every leaf and blade hung a dewdrop that turned into a diamond in the sunlight. It looked as if a shower of brillants had fallen. As the sun rose higher, they disappeared one by one; they went to freshen the roots as they had refreshed the foliage. That set me thinking, and from thinking I fell to rhyming thus:

> Lou diaman briia san n' èstr 'utilé,
> Se briian san faïré maï,
> Sèn coumma l' estèla qué fila,
> Que fila, fila, é sen vaï.
> Mè se pendèn nosta carriièra,
> Sèn utiles tout en briian,
> Avan d' intra din la poussiièra,
> Aouren fa un traval bèn gran'.*

With great earnestness and a slight quaver in his voice, my white-haired grandfather had uttered those few lines of poetry.

We were all silent, and not a sound could be heard save the crackling of the olive-tree leaves in the fireplace and the monotonous tick of the big clock on the landing of the stone stairs.

> *The diamonds useless shine,
> Man strives for glitter-gains.
> Like shooting-stars we fall—
> A flash, and that is all.
> So let us shape our course
> For better, not for worse,
> And snow and shine combine
> With deed and work divine.

With uplifted eyes we gazed on the bent form and benign face of our story-teller, who with clasped hands pensively watched the ascending sparks in the huge chimney.

Suddenly the old clock groaned; there was a rumbling of wheels, and the sound of the bell majestically swelled in the long corridor and ran from arch to arch of the vaulted room. At the same moment, the old cock in the barnyard sent his lusty crowing out into the starry night.

Those two familiar sounds drew my grandfather out of his reverie; and with a smile I would fain reproduce, and a twinkle from his deeply-set hazel brown eyes, he said:

"Lou Gal cantè, é moun vouiiage finiguè."*

* The cock crew and my journey ended.

Other titles from
THE HIPPOCRENE LIBRARY OF FOLKLORE . . .

Czech, Moravian and Slovak Fairy Tales
Parker Fillmore

Everyone loves a "Story that Never Ends". . . Such is aptly titled the very last story in this authentic collection of Czech, Moravian and Slovak fairy tales, that will charm readers young and old alike. Fifteen different classic, regional folk tales and 23 charming illustrations whisk the reader to places of romance, deception, royalty, and magic. "The Betrothal Gifts," "Grandfather's Eyes," and "The Golden Spinning-Wheel" are a few examples of the enchanting stories that make this collection of fairy tales a beautiful addition to any library.
Ages 12 and up
243 pages • 23 b/w illustrations • 5 1/2 x 8 1/4 • 0-7818-0714-X • W • $14.95 hc • (792)

Fairy Gold: A Book of Classic English Fairy Tales
Chosen by Ernest Rhys
Illustrated by Herbert Cole

"The Fairyland which you enter, through the golden door of this book, is pictured in tales and rhymes that have been told at one time or another to English children," begins this charming volume of favorite English fairy tales. Forty-nine imaginative black and white illustrations accompany thirty classic tales, including such beloved stories as "Jack and the Bean Stalk," "The Three Bears," and "Chicken Licken" (Chicken Little to American audiences).
Ages 12 and up
236 pages 5 1/2 x 8 1/4 • 49 b/w illustrations • 0-7818-0700-X • W • $14.95hc • (790)

Folk Tales from Bohemia
Adolf Wenig
This folk tale collection is one of a kind, focusing uniquely on humankind's struggle with evil in the world. Delicately ornate red and black text and illustrations set the mood. "How the Devil Contended with Man," "The Devil's Gifts," and "How an Old Woman Cheated the Devil" are just 2 of 9 suspenseful folk tales which interweave good and evil, magic and reality, struggle and conquest.
Ages 9 and up
98 pages • red and black illustrations • 5 1/2 x 8 1/4 • 0-7818-0718-2 • W • $14.95hc • (786)

Folk Tales from Chile
Brenda Hughes
This selection of 15 tales gives a taste of the variety of Chile's rich folklore. There is a story of the spirit who lived in a volcano and kept his daughter imprisoned in the mountain, guarded by a devoted dwarf; there are domestic tales with luck favoring the poor and simple, and tales which tell how poppies first appeared in the cornfields and how the Big Stone in Lake Llanquihue came to be there. Fifteen charming illustrations accompany the text.
Ages 7 and up
121 pages • 5 1/2 x 8 1/4 • 15 illustrations • 0-7818-0712-3 • W • $12.50hc • (785)

Folk Tales from Russia
by Donald A. Mackenzie
From Hippocrene's classic folklore series comes this collection of short stories of myth, fable, and adventure—all infused with the rich and varied cultural identity of Russia. With nearly 200 pages and 8 full-page black-and-white illustrations, the reader will be charmed by these legendary folk tales that symbolically weave magical fantasy with the historic events of Russia's past.
Ages 12 and up
192 pages • 8 b/w illustrations • 5 1/2 x 8 1/4 • 0-7818-0696-8 • W • $12.50hc • (788)

Folk Tales from Simla
Alice Elizabeth Dracott
From Simla, once the summer capital of India under British rule, comes a charming collection of Himalayan folk lore, known for its beauty, wit, and mysticism. These 56 stories, fire-side tales of the hill-folk of Northern India, will surely enchant readers of all ages. Eight illustrations by the author complete this delightful volume.
Ages 12 and up
225 pages • 5 1/2 x 8 1/4 • 8 illustrations • 0-7818-0704-2 • W • $14.95hc • (794)

Glass Mountain: Twenty-Eight Ancient Polish Folk Tales and Fables
W.S. Kuniczak
Illustrated by Pat Bargielski
As a child in a far-away misty corner of Volhynia, W.S. Kuniczak was carried away to an extraordinary world of magic and illusion by the folk tales of his Polish nurse. "To this day I merely need to close my eyes to see . . . an imaginary picture show and chart the marvelous geography of the fantastic," he writes in his introduction.
171 pages • 6 x 9 • 8 illustrations • 0-7818-0552-X • W • $16.95hc • (645)

The Little Mermaid and Other Tales
Hans Christian Andersen
Here is a near replica of the first American edition of 27 classic fairy tales from the masterful Hans Christian Andersen. Children and adults alike will enjoy timeless favorites including "The Little Mermaid," "The Emperor's New Clothes," "The Little Matchgirl," and "The Ugly Duckling." These stories, and many more, whisk the reader to magical lands, fantastic voyages, romantic encounters, and suspenseful adventures. Beautiful black-and-white sketches enhance these fairy tales and bring them to life.
Ages 9 and up
508 pages • color, b/w illustrations • 6 x 9 • 0-7818-0720-4 • W • $19.95hc • (791)

Old Polish Legends
Retold by F.C. Anstruther
Wood engravings by J. Sekalski
Now available in a new gift edition! This fine collection of eleven fairy tales, with an introduction by Zymunt Nowakowski, was first published in Scotland during World War II, when the long night of the German occupation was at its darkest. The tales, however, "recall the ancient beautiful times, to laugh and to weep . . ."
66 pages • 7 1/4 x 9 • 11 woodcut engravings • 0-78180521-X • W • $11.95hc • (653)

Pakistani Folk Tales: Toontoony Pie and Other Stories
Ashraf Siddiqui and Marilyn Lerch
Illustrated by Jan Fairservis
In this collection of 22 folk tales set in Pakistan, are found not only the familiar figures of folklore—kings and beautiful princesses—but the magic of the Far East, cunning jackals, and wise holy men. Thirty-eight charming illustrations by Jan Fairservis complete this enchanting collection.
Ages 7 and up
158 pages • 6 x 9 • 38 illustrations • 0-7818-0703-4 • W • $12.50hc • (784)

Polish Fables: Bilingual Edition
Ignacy Krasicki
Translated by Gerard T. Kapolka
Ignacy Krasicki (1735-1801) was hailed as "The Prince of Poets" by his contemporaries. With great artistry the author used contemporary events and human relations to show a course to guide human conduct. For over two centuries, Krasicki's fables have entertained and instructed his delighted readers. This bilingual gift edition contains the original Polish text with side-by side English translation. Twenty illustrations by Barbara Swidzinska , a well known Polish artist, add to the volume's charm.
105 pages • 6 x 9 • 20 illustrations • 0-7818-0548-1 • W • $19.95hc • (646)

Swedish Fairy Tales

Translated by H. L. Braekstad A unique blending of enchantment, adventure, comedy, and romance make this collection of Swedish fairy tales a must-have for any library. With 18 different, classic Swedish fairy tales and 21 beautiful black-and-white illustrations, this is an ideal gift for children and adults alike.
Ages 9 and up
190 pages • 21 b/w illustrations • 5 1/2 x 8 1/4 • 0-7818-0717-4 • W • $12.50hc • (787)

Twenty Scottish Tales and Legends

Edited by Cyril Swinson
Illustrated by Allan Stewart
Twenty enchanting myths take the reader to an extraordinary world of magic harps, angry giants, mysterious spells and gallant Knights. Amusingly divided into sections such as Tales of Battle and Pursuit, Kings and Conquests, and Tales of Daring, this book brings to life the legendary Scottish mythology of ages past. Eight detailed illustrations by Allan Stewart bring the beauty of the Scottish countryside to the collection.
Ages 9 and up
215 pages • 5 1/2 x 8 1/4 • 8 b/w illustrations • 0-7818-0701-8 • W • $12.50hc • (789)

All prices subject to change. **To purchase Hippocrene Books** contact your local bookstore, call (718) 454-2366, or write to: HIPPOCRENE BOOKS, 171 Madison Avenue, New York, NY 10016. Please enclose check or money order, adding $5.00 shipping (UPS) for the first book and $.50 for each additional book.